An Appeal for Justice: The Trials of the Scottsboro Nine

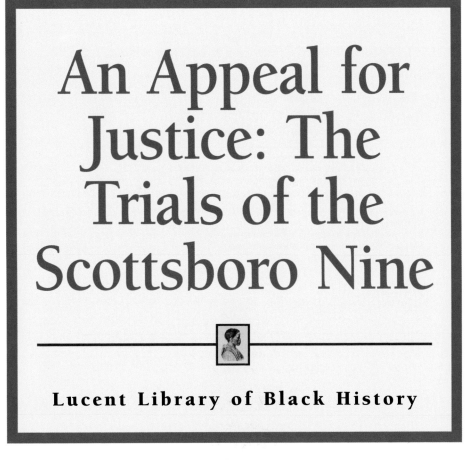

Lucent Library of Black History

John F. Wukovits

LUCENT BOOKS
A part of Gale, Cengage Learning

GALE
CENGAGE Learning·

Detroit • New York • San Francisco • New Haven, Conn • Waterville, Maine • London

LIBRARY OF CONGRESS CATALOGING-IN-PUBLICATION DATA

Wukovits, John F., 1944-
  An appeal for justice : the trials of the Scottsboro Nine / by John F. Wukovits.
     p. cm. -- (Lucent library of Black history)
  Includes bibliographical references and index.
  ISBN 978-1-4205-0676-1 (hardcover)
  1. Trials (Rape)--Alabama--Scottsboro. [1. Scottsboro Trial, Scottsboro, Ala., 1931.] I. Title.
  KF224.S34W85 2012
  345.761'9502523--dc23
                                                    2011029200

Lucent Books
27500 Drake Rd.
Farmington Hills, MI 48331

ISBN-13: 978-1-4205-0676-1
ISBN-10: 1-4205-0676-5

Printed in the United States of America
2 3 4 5 6 7 15 14 13 12

Contents

Foreword

It has been more than 500 years since Africans were first brought to the New World in shackles, and over 140 years since slavery was formally abolished in the United States. Over 50 years have passed since the fallacy of "separate but equal" was obliterated in the American courts, and some 40 years since the watershed Civil Rights Act of 1965 guaranteed the rights and liberties of all Americans, especially those of color. Over time, these changes have become celebrated landmarks in American history. In the twenty-first century, African American men and women are politicians, judges, diplomats, professors, deans, doctors, artists, athletes, business owners, and home owners. For many, the scars of the past have melted away in the opportunities that have been found in contemporary society. Observers such as Peter N. Kirsanow, who sits on the U.S. Commission of Civil Rights, point to these accomplishments and conclude, "The growing black middle class may be viewed as proof that most of the civil rights battles have been won."

In spite of these legal victories, however, prejudice and inequality have persisted in American society. In 2003, African Americans comprised just 12 percent of the nation's population, yet accounted for 44 percent of its prison inmates and 24 percent of its poor. Racially motivated hate crimes continue to appear on the pages of major newspapers in many American cities. Furthermore, many African Americans still experience either overt or muted racism in their daily lives. A 1996 study undertaken by Professor Nancy Krieger of the Harvard School of Public Health, for example, found that 80 percent of the African American participants reported having experienced racial discrimination in one or more settings, including at work or school, applying for housing and medical care, from the police or in the courts, and on the street or in a public setting.

It is for these reasons that many believe the struggle for racial equality and justice is far from over. These episodes of discrimination threaten to shatter the illusion that America has completely overcome its racist past, causing many black Americans to become increasingly frustrated and confused. Scholar and writer Ellis Cose has described this splintered state in the following way: "I have done everything I was supposed to do. I have stayed out of trouble with the law, gone to the right schools, and worked myself nearly to death. What more do they want? Why in God's name won't they accept me as a full human being?" For Cose and others, the struggle for equality and justice has yet to be fully achieved.

In many subtle yet important ways the traumatic experiences of slavery and segregation continue to inform the way race is discussed and experienced in the twenty-first century. Indeed, it is possible that America will always grapple with the fallout from its distressing past. Ulric Haynes, dean of the Hofstra University School of Business has said, "Perhaps race will always matter, given the historical circumstances under which we came to this country." But studying this past and understanding how it contributes to present-day dialogues about race and history in America is a critical component of contemporary education. To this end, the Lucent Library of Black History offers a thorough look at the experiences that have shaped the black community and the American people as a whole. Annotated bibliographies provide readers with ideas for further research, while fully documented primary and secondary source quotations enhance the text. Each book in the series explores a different episode of black history; together they provide students with a wealth of information as well as launching points for further study and discussion.

A Different System

The racial situation that existed in the United States of the 1930s vastly differed from what prevails today. In today's post-civil-rights era, equal rights have been affirmed for African Americans, and black men and women have made strides in achieving equality with whites. Some have stepped into powerful positions in medicine, business, entertainment, and other fields, including the presidency.

In the South of the 1930s few avenues were open to black citizens. Instead of enjoying equal opportunities, blacks lived in the shadows of a world dominated and run exclusively by whites. Whites throughout the South dominated not only businesses, but controlled the police, the courts, and local and state governments. Nowhere among those posts in the South would one find a black person in authority.

Thus some readers today, accustomed to a fairer social and economic system, might find it difficult to understand how nine innocent blacks could be callously rounded up, tried, and convicted on little more than the word of two white women. That, however, was the norm in the first half of the twentieth century. In the South at that time any black male accused of raping a white female could expect, at best, a trial and conviction in a court of law; at worst he would be hanged. Few whites were troubled by this lack of justice for African Americans, and those who may have objected remained largely silent out of fear of retribution from racist whites.

This situation had existed since the end of the U.S. Civil War in 1865. After the war, during a period called Reconstruction (1865–1877), African Americans enjoyed a period of protection by the federal government and relative equality with their white neighbors. However, as time passed and federal troops left the South, white southerners reinforced their dominance. A new way of living appeared in which blacks, while legally free, lived in abject poverty in a system run and controlled by whites, many of

In the 1930s a "separate but equal" system had evolved in the South that restricted African Americans from crossing the boundary between the white and black worlds. Above all, they were denied the civil rights enjoyed by white Americans.

whom had once been slave owners. Former slaves who could find no work in the postwar world often returned to the plantations to labor for their former bosses. There they entered into an arrangement called sharecropping: In exchange for simple living quarters and meager pay, they worked the same fields they had tilled as slaves. While they theoretically lived as free men and women on equal terms with whites, in actuality they lived outside the fringes of white society in an inferior world created and maintained by the bigotry of that white society.

Organizations such as the Ku Klux Klan (KKK) devoted themselves to maintaining white supremacy and keeping the former slaves in poverty. The KKK attracted many whites and relied on violence and threats to keep the blacks "in their place." They operated in secrecy, masking their identities beneath white hoods and robes, but their activities were condoned by much of white society.

Gradually an official system evolved featuring two separate, but certainly not equal, societies—white and black. African Americans were restricted from many basic freedoms. Blacks were strictly forbidden to cross the boundaries separating the two worlds, and in the 1930s few things were considered more heinous by white southern society than a black male physically attacking a white female.

This was the situation in the South for nine young black men traveling by the rails in 1931. In a blink of an eye their lives altered dramatically and tragically. In the long process that followed, these nine young men, supported by keen-minded lawyers and others who took up their cause, helped solidify equal rights for everyone and contributed to the birth of the civil rights movement led by Martin Luther King Jr. in the 1950s.

Chapter One

A Tragic Train Ride

The nine young men who would become known as the Scottsboro Boys never expected the train ride to end as it did. They had hopped aboard one of the open cargo cars without purchasing a ticket. Although this was illegal, thousands of unemployed people, mostly men, traveled this way during the Great Depression of the 1930s. At the time they were called hobos. They hoped to find work at one of the towns along the way, a hot meal or two, and put a few dollars in their pockets. Instead, on this trip, a nightmarish scenario unfolded, and nine young men all wound up in jail surrounded by an angry crowd screaming for their lives.

Fight on a Train

The nine, including eighteen-year-old Haywood Patterson, rested in one of the open gondolas as the train crossed into Alabama from Tennessee on March 25, 1931. When a white male also riding the train with some friends stepped on Patterson's hand in trying to cross to the other boxcar, Patterson objected. In moments the two groups began shouting at each other, calling each other names. According to another of the black riders, Clarence Norris, when the whites hurled gravel toward the

From 1882 to 1932 over three thousand African Americans were lynched by white mobs, without benefit of a trial.

blacks and shouted, "All you n****** unload, get your asses offa here," an all-out brawl ensued. A few travelers remained in the background, preferring not to fight or deciding the affair was none of their business. Within minutes the blacks had forced the white men they were fighting with to jump off the moving train, and, according to Norris, "when they hit the ground they would tumble quite a ways."[1] One of their foes, Orville Gilley, slipped as he tried to jump from the train and perilously clung to the side of the car while the tracks sped by below. One of the blacks, fearing Gilley might be killed if he lost his grip, reached down and helped him back into the gondola as the train picked up speed.

The nine blacks were aware of the dangers of traveling in the Deep South, where many white southerners considered black

Northern View of the South

Hollace Ransdell, a reporter hired by the American Civil Liberties Union (ACLU) to investigate the attitudes in Scottsboro, uncovered what to her and the ACLU were near-unbelievable opinions that southern whites held of southern blacks. In her report to the organization, Ransdell pulled no punches.

> Strolling around observing these things, it is hard to conceive that anything but kindly feelings and gentle manners toward all mankind can stir the hearts of the citizens of Scottsboro. It came as a shock, therefore, to see these pleasant faces stiffen, these laughing mouths grow narrow and sinister, those soft eyes become cold and hard because the question was mentioned of a fair trial for nine young Negroes terrified and quite alone. Suddenly these kindly-looking mouths were saying the most frightful things. To see people who ordinarily would be gentle and compassionate at the thought of a child—a white one—in the least trouble, who would wince at the sight of a suffering dog—to see these men and women transformed by blind, unreasoning antipathy so that their lips parted and their eyes glowed with lust for the blood of black children, was a sight to make one untouched by the spell of violent prejudice shrink.

Hollace Ransdell. "Report on the Scottsboro, Ala. Case." American Civil Liberties Union, May 27, 1931, p. 18. www.law.umkc.edu/faculty/projects/FTrials/scottsboro/Scottsbororeport.pdf.

Northerners were shocked by the antipathy displayed by southern whites toward African Americans.

Americans inferior and treated them harshly. The southern states passed a series of laws, called Jim Crow laws, that severely restricted the rights of African Americans. Blacks had to use separate water fountains, attend their own schools, and even had to step off the sidewalk when a white person approached. Should a black person object to these laws, he was likely to be badly beaten or even taken to a nearby tree and hanged, an illegal act called lynching. From 1882 to 1932, more than three thousand blacks had been lynched in the South.

Whites had a deeply ingrained belief that blacks were inferior to whites. The South's economy, once built upon plantation cotton and rice, thrived in the eighteenth and first half of the nineteenth centuries, but it was one dependent upon slaves to perform the hard labor. Brought forcibly to the country from Africa along the infamous Middle Passage across the Atlantic Ocean, slaves became an essential component of the Southern economy. In this system black slaves were bought and sold as property to work the fields and serve the whites. The slaves did not have any rights and were not treated as humans.

Some people in the nation, called abolitionists, objected to slavery on the grounds that it was not only immoral, but also unconstitutional. During the American Civil War (1861–1865) between the North and the South, President Abraham Lincoln emancipated the slaves held in Southern-controlled areas, an act bitterly resented in the South. Though the former slaves had been legally granted full equality in the 1860s, by the 1930s they had yet to exercise those rights or to be integrated into southern society.

Arrested

The whites who were forced off the train did not intend to let the slight go unanswered. They ran to the nearby town of Stevenson, Alabama, and told the depot manager there that a gang of blacks had attacked them. The depot manager in turn called ahead to the train station at Paint Rock and told them to remove the blacks when the train stopped there. Jackson County deputy sheriff Charlie Latham received a call from his superior, Sheriff M.L. Wann, ordering him to deputize every white male he could gather in Paint Rock, to seize all black passengers on the train, and to transport them to Scottsboro, a few miles away. Latham organized his temporary posse, all armed with rifles, and lined them along both sides of the track leading into Paint Rock.

As the train pulled into Paint Rock, the blacks riding the train stared at the group of armed men waiting to board and realized the predicament they faced. Within ten minutes Latham's group had searched all forty-two cars and detained the nine blacks aboard, tied them together, and placed them on the back of a truck for transport to Scottsboro. The posse also found Gilley and two white women, Victoria Price and Ruby Bates, in the same gondola. The sheriff ordered them taken to Scottsboro as witnesses of the alleged assault.

The two women had been riding the train for the same reason as the men—searching for work. In the South in those days, their presence among the men, especially several black men, would have been seen as highly inappropriate and may have been questioned by the authorities. Any questions the authorities may have had for the women were forgotten when the women accused the nine black males of raping them.

Many of the white deputies wanted to lynch the nine on the spot for a crime that southern society considered worse than any other—sexual assault of a white female by a black male—but Latham refused to budge. He told his men they had to follow the law and transport the accused safely to the Scottsboro jail.

The men arrested ranged in age from 13 to 20 and had traveled in two groups. Four lived in Chattanooga, Tennessee—Patterson, age 18; 19-year-old Andy Wright and his brother Roy, age 13; and Eugene Williams, age 13. The other five came from various towns in Georgia—Norris, age 18; Charlie Weems, age 20; Ozie Powell, age 15; Olen Montgomery, age 19; and Willie Roberson, age 15.

The nine shared common stories. Most had endured difficult childhoods, dropped out of school before junior high, and had held odd jobs wherever they could find them. Roberson suffered from syphilis, a sexually transmitted disease that produces a variety of painful symptoms, including sores in the genital area, hair loss, fever, rashes, and skin lesions. Montgomery's eyesight was so poor he was nearly blind. Powell registered an intelligence quotient (IQ) of just 64.

Throughout the South the nine came to be called the Scottsboro Boys. No matter the age, black males at that time were called

The young black men who would become known as the "Scottsboro Nine" are shown after their arrest. They were alleged to have raped two white women.

"boy" by white society until they reached an advanced age, when they were called "uncle."

Price and Bates had also lived hard lives. Poorly educated, they had sporadically worked in Huntsville's cotton mills and lived in wooden shacks with their parents. Bates's family lived in a black section of town. Price, who seemed to enjoy the attention the case brought her, was known as a prostitute and heavy drinker.

Emotions Intensify

While a physician examined both girls in Scottsboro, news of the alleged assault spread throughout the region. Exaggerated versions circulated, and a crowd began gathering outside the jail, growing larger and angrier by the hour as carloads and truckloads of people flocked to the scene. A local newspaper reporter needed five minutes just to work his way through the crowd and reach the jail.

As nightfall approached, hostility increased. Wann thought of taking the prisoners to a stronger jail at Etowah, but someone had cut the wires in the three available cars to make sure they would not work. "Bring them damn n****** out,"[2] shouted some from the throng, who threatened to break in and drag the nine out. Despite personally knowing many of the people in the crowd, the sheriff did not hesitate to enforce the law. He pulled his weapon and shouted back, "If you come any further, I'll blow your damn brains out. There ain't nobody coming in here. If you try, if you put your feet in this door, I'm gonna blow your brains out."[3]

The sheriff's courageous stand against his neighbors and friends saved the prisoners' lives that night. However, Wann knew he needed reinforcement if he was to prevent a lynching, so around 9:00 P.M. he telephoned Alabama governor Benjamin Miller and asked for assistance. Miller, who had long campaigned against lynching, ordered Major Joseph Starnes to lead his detachment of twenty-five National Guard soldiers stationed at Guntersville the twenty miles to Scottsboro and establish order. By midnight Starnes had arrived and posted a cordon of men around the Scottsboro jail. For the moment, anyway, the National Guard restored a semblance of calm.

While the National Guard maintained order outside, inside the jail the nine prisoners worried about their fates. Would the Guard, composed of armed white males, turn on the captives at the behest of the crowd, or would it continue to follow orders and protect the prisoners? Growing up in the South, each of the accused had been abused by police in the past or knew someone who had, and with people outside shouting for their blood, they wondered how long the Guard would hold out. "I believed the National Guard was some part of the lynching bee," says Patterson.

"When they came into my cell I figured like the others—that we were as good as long gone now."[4]

The National Guard held true to their duty. The *Huntsville Times*, the local newspaper, explained their predicament. "Officers had to point guns at friends to keep them away from black men they themselves would have been glad to get to."[5] They put aside personal concerns to carry out their responsibilities, in the process saving the lives of nine terrified young men.

A Pleasant Town

The tiny town of Scottsboro, Alabama, was usually a quiet, serene place. Twenty miles south of the Tennessee border, Scottsboro, the county seat of Jackson County, was a quaint village of thirty-five hundred inhabitants. According to Hollace Ransdell, an investigator sent to Scottsboro by the American Civil Liberties Union (ACLU), it was

> situated in the midst of pleasant rolling hills. Neat, well-tended farms lie all around, the deep red of their soil making a striking contrast with the rich green of the hills. The cottages of the town stand back on soft lawns, shaded with handsome trees. A feeling of peace and leisure is in the air. The people on the streets have easy kind faces and greet strangers as well as each other cordially. In the Courthouse Square in the center of town, the village celebrities, such as the mayor, the sheriff, the lawyers, lounge and chat democratically with the town eccentrics and plain citizens.[6]

The citizens liked tradition and familiarity. Mayor James Snodgrass held that town's top political office almost every year since 1884, and the town's appearance, other than a repainting here and there, had changed little since the turn of the century. A black section of town stood apart from the more prosperous white section. Townspeople flocked to the courthouse and surrounding town square, with its attractive gazebo where bands performed concerts, for social occasions as well as to conduct business. Farmers from the adjoining area drove to Scottsboro to meet with each other, swap farm techniques, discuss the impact of the economic depression that swamped the nation, and enjoy a leisurely day in the sun.

Southern View of the South

While much of the country hastened to condemn the southern courts and social systems, many people who lived in the South defended their way of life. On April 14, 1931, the *Montgomery Advertiser* printed an editorial stating that while the evidence clearly showed that the nine had raped the women, "Yet over the country there will be many people who cannot believe this and who will carry that prejudice ruled. This is not the truth; these negroes were given every protection and every right of the law for defense; their own evidence was so conflicting that the attorneys trying their best to defend their lives were almost helpless to aid them." The editorial ended by reaffirming that justice was done. "Jackson County wanted to do what was right; as a citizenry composed of people who hold inviolate its women, it offers no apology to the rest of the country for the penalty imposed upon these blacks who would, according to the evidence, be a dangerous menace to any section of any country in the world."

Quoted in James R. Acker. *Scottsboro and Its Legacy.* Westport, CT: Praeger, 2008, p. 37.

The pleasant locale served as a stop along the train route of the Alabama Great Southern Railroad coming down into the state from Chattanooga, Tennessee. It also possessed a jailhouse. Because it did, Scottsboro became the stage for one of the most emotional legal dramas played out in the nation.

The Nine Are Accused

In Scottsboro the next day, Latham placed the nine accused males in a lineup and asked the women to identify their attackers. Price walked by each of the accused and pointed to six as her assailants, one by one, but Bates at first remained silent. "If those six had Miss Price," blurted a jail guard, "it stands to reason that the others had Miss Bates."[7] Bates did not contradict the guard's assumption, but observers noticed her reluctance to step forward and accuse anyone, as opposed to Price's obvious willingness to bring charges.

The next day Price took her story to the press by saying to a reporter, "When I saw them nab those Negroes, I sure was happy.

Victoria Price (left) and Ruby Bates were the alleged rape victims in the Scottsboro case.

Mister, I never had a break in my life. Those Negroes have ruined me and Ruby forever. The only thing I ask is that they give them all the law allows."[8] Observers and members of the press noticed that Price seemed to enjoy being the center of attention.

Gilley, the white traveler who had not been forced off the gondola, added that he witnessed the rapes and that all nine had been involved. He said that during the crime one of the accused pointed a pistol at him while another held a knife against his ribs to make certain he would not interfere. Authorities willingly accepted a story that backed Price and overlooked a discrepancy in their stories; Price claimed twelve blacks had boarded the car, Gilley said he saw only nine.

The nine black males reacted with disbelief after the lineup. Norris called the girls liars, causing a guard to strike him with his bayonet with such force that it sliced the skin to the bone. "I was scared before," Norris admitted later, "but it wasn't nothing to how I felt now. I knew if a white woman accused a black man of rape, he was as good as dead."[9]

Thirteen-year-old Roy Wright so feared for his life that he laid blame for the event at the feet of five of the other men. He told police that he and the three with whom he was traveling had done nothing. None of the other eight made such charges against the others at this time. Afterward, Wright claimed he made this accusation out of an extreme fear for his life.

The two town newspapers added to the emotions by printing stories that cast the nine as criminals and the girls as innocent victims. The *Progressive Age* stated that the details of what area citizens called the "n***** rape case" were "too revolting to be printed,"[10] while the *Jackson County Sentinel* posted a headline which left little doubt where the paper stood. "Nine Black Fiends Committed Revolting Crime," it stated, with text adding that police found the two girls "in a terrible condition mentally and physically after their unspeakable experience at the hands of the black brutes."[11] The papers reflected the feelings held by the white community, not only in Scottsboro but also much of Alabama and the South.

Wann had his doubts about the truth of the accusations and told Patterson that he did not believe the girls. He asked the National Guard to transport the men to nearby Gadsden, where Wann thought the nine would be safer than if they remained in Scottsboro. Again, the National Guard followed orders, causing Norris to later state, "The Guard was with us every step of the way or we never would have made it."[12] In the meantime, Wann held the two girls in Scottsboro as material witnesses to the crimes.

Preparation for Trial

Legal representation had to be arranged for the nine accused, but few lawyers in the region—all of whom were white—were willing to accept the case. The local judge finally persuaded sixty-nine-year-old Milo C. Moody to defend the accused. The prisoners were hardly reassured by the thought that an aging white lawyer was all that stood between them and the electric chair. According to investigator Ransdell, who met the lawyer at the time, Moody was a "doddering, extremely unreliable, senile individual who is losing whatever ability he once had."[13]

Sixty miles away one of Chattanooga, Tennessee's leading black physicians, Dr. P.A. Stephens, tried to help with legal issues. He organized a group of concerned African American citizens and raised money to hire local attorney Stephen R. Roddy to go to Scottsboro and team with Moody to defend the young men. Unfortunately Roddy, an alcoholic who had been jailed the year before for public drunkenness, was little better than his cohort.

The prisoners needed all the help they could get, however. The American Civil Liberties Union (ACLU), an organization devoted to fighting for those whose rights are threatened, had commissioned Ransdell to travel to Scottsboro, interview local citizens to gauge the mood of the region, and check into the backgrounds of all the principal characters in the drama. In a lengthy report she wrote after she finished her investigation, Ransdell concluded that the Scottsboro Nine had been judged guilty before the trial began and wrote of the officials and citizens with whom she discussed the case,

> They all wanted the Negroes killed as quickly as possible in a way that would not bring disrepute upon the town. They therefore preferred a sentence of death by a judge, to a sentence of death by a mob, but they desired the same result, and were impatient with anything that slowed up the

conviction and death sentence which they all knew was coming regardless of any testimony.[14]

Ransdell added that this desire for execution emerged from long-set, misguided notions about the inferiority of blacks.

> They said that all negroes were brutes and had to be held down by stern repressive measures or the number of rapes on white women would be larger than it is. Their point seemed to be that it was only by ruthless oppression of the Negro that any white woman was able to escape raping at Negro hands. Starting with this notion, it followed that they could not conceive that two white girls found riding with a crowd of Negroes could possibly have escaped raping. A Negro will always, in their opinion, rape a white woman if he gets the chance.[15]

Ransdell quoted one southerner in Scottsboro who bluntly expressed the prevalent attitude. "We white people just couldn't afford to let these N****** get off because of the effect it would have on other N******."[16]

On Monday, March 30, the all-white Jackson County grand jury listened to evidence concerning the case. The following day, to no one's surprise the grand jury charged each of the nine young men with rape and set a trial for April 6, only one week away. "Surrounded by a cordon of soldiers bristling with automatic rifles, pistols, and riot guns," wrote the *Jackson County Sentinel* the day after the grand jury completed its business, "nine negro men stood up in the Jackson County courthouse last Tuesday morning and were indicted on the most serious charges known on the statute books of Alabama—rape."[17]

Patterson, Weems, Roy Wright, and the other accused understood the seriousness of the charges. They had already endured more than a week of slurs and death threats from an angry mob that had only been prevented from killing them by the National Guard. They had been separated from family and lived in tiny jail cells. Now, standing beside lawyers in whom they placed little confidence, they listened as the grand jury issued a conclusion that would send them to trial on rape charges and most likely result in death sentences.

Under the system that had evolved in the South following the Civil War, a black man could be arrested for simply staring at a white female for too long. This crime was called "reckless eye-balling." Accusations of rape were punished severely. Most African Americans had heard of the 1923 incident in Rosewood, Florida, when white males burned down the town and killed six blacks after a white female claimed a black man from Rosewood had raped her. The Scottsboro Nine now heard their names mentioned by a grand jury that seemed all too eager to send them to trial. The Alabama legal system set the sentence for rape at anywhere ranging from ten years in prison to death in the electric chair, but they had little doubt, unless a miracle of some sort occurred, what fate awaited them.

Chapter Two

The First Round of Trials

The arrests and detention of the Scottsboro Nine featured harsh handling by guards and the menace of imminent harm or even death at the hands of a rowdy crowd. Those perils continued as people gathered for the trials, but a new element appeared. The crowd in Scottsboro seemed to be enjoying the spectacle as if they were attending a circus instead of a trial to determine the fates of nine young men.

The Trials Begin

The trial opened on Monday, April 6, 1931. For decades the inhabitants around Scottsboro had gathered in the town on the first Monday of each month for "Fair Day," a time when farmers and their families came into town from the outlying regions. For an entire day, a mixture of agricultural business and fun unfolded, offering a break in the tedium of scraping out a living during the Depression. Farmers traded produce while wives and children socialized.

While the sounds of commerce and laughter filled Scottsboro, a detachment of the National Guard brought the nine defendants from Gadsden and locked them in the county jail until they would be needed at the courthouse. By 10:00 A.M. a crowd

The prisoners needed National Guardsmen to escort them from the jailhouse to the courtroom, due to the vicious racial taunting and the constant threat of violence from the crowds outside the courthouse.

estimated at eight thousand had clogged the main avenues, many eagerly awaiting the appearance of the accused.

When the National Guard troops began walking the prisoners from the jail to the courthouse, a raucous crowd peppered their trek with insults and threats. "You n****** gonna die," they shouted at the nine. "Your black asses gonna burn. The electric chair's too good for you bastards."[18] People cursed Stephen R. Roddy when he first appeared but then chuckled when the lawyer, who had obviously been drinking, had difficulty walking a straight line.

The young men's lawyers, Roddy and Milo C. Moody, met with the prosecution, the team of lawyers that would argue for the state and try to convince the jury that a crime had been committed. Circuit Solicitor H.G. Bailey, the lead prosecution attorney, assumed Roddy would ask for a separate trial for each of the nine defendants, but Roddy agreed to try them together. Bailey, convinced that the nine men had varying levels of involvement in the event on the train, worried that such a move would lead to a mistrial by a reviewing judge. He suggested they try the men in four groups, beginning with Clarence Norris and Charlie Weems, against whom the prosecution felt they had the strongest cases, and ending with that of the youngest defendant, Roy Wright. When Roddy expressed no objections, the lawyers left to prepare for the trial's opening.

Roddy hurriedly met with his clients just before the trial for their lives began. He told the group that if they were honest with him, he might be able to prevent their executions, but the nine doubted his abilities. The prospect of going into a court and arguing their cases to an all-white jury seemed to frighten Roddy, whose breath smelled of alcohol. Hollace Ransdell thought he looked intimidated by the crowd, the National Guard, the judge, and everything else about the trial.

The National Guard posted men with machine guns at every door and kept the crowd 100 feet (30.48m) from the courthouse to maintain order. Before a packed courtroom of spectators from which all females and all males under the age of twenty-one had been barred, Judge Alfred E. Hawkins called the court to order. When he asked Roddy if he was representing the nine accused, Roddy gave a confusing answer in which he at first stated he was not and that he was unfamiliar with Alabama law, and then said he was their lawyer. Moody replied in the affirmative.

Roddy and Moody first asked for a change of venue which, if granted, would switch the trial to another city where passions might not be as inflamed against the accused. They argued that local newspaper coverage made a fair trial almost impossible, and the presence of the National Guard emphasized the danger the nine faced from the town's inhabitants. The prosecution responded that the crowd outside had simply gathered out of curiosity, not because they intended to harm anyone. Hawkins agreed with the prosecution and ordered the trial to proceed.

Day One

Wearing a new dress, Victoria Price took the witness stand to open the trial of Norris and Weems. She stated that on March 24 she and Ruby Bates left Huntsville seeking work in Chattanooga's cotton mills. When they found nothing, they again hopped a train to return home, riding with seven white males in a gondola when suddenly twelve black males jumped into the car. Two sported pistols and all flashed knives as they ordered the white males off the train. Price added that Norris then propositioned her. When Price refused, she said six of the black men overpowered her. She identified Weems, Norris, both Andy and Roy Wright, Haywood Patterson, and Olen Montgomery as the men who raped her, ignoring her pleas to stop. In his cross-examination Roddy attempted to introduce evidence on Price's sordid reputation, but Hawkins refused to allow it. Such information is often considered irrelevant in a rape trial.

According to some reports, Price appeared to enjoy being the center of attention. She delivered her explanations in a firm, assured voice, and answered Roddy's questions with a disdain that endeared her to the packed courtroom. "She did it with such gusto, snap and wise-cracks, that the courtroom was often in a roar of laughter,"

Victoria Price

———■———

Born in 1911, Victoria Price, who grew up in the poor section of Huntsville, Alabama, worked in local cotton mills as a spinner when ten years old. She supported her infirm mother but could not make enough from the cotton mill to adequately provide for both her mother and herself. She later supplemented her income by turning to prostitution, selling herself to white and black males alike, according to some reports. She traveled the South often as a hobo, sleeping at night in hobo encampments called jungles.

After the trials ended, Price faded into obscurity until 1976, when she was found living in Tennessee. Price died in 1982.

reported Ransdell. "Her flip retorts to the attorney for the defense, Steven Roddy, especially caused amusement."[19] Ransdell added,

> The talk with Victoria Price, particularly, convinced me that she was the type who welcomes attention and publicity at any price. The price in this case meant little to her, as she has no notions of shame connected with sexual intercourse in any form and was quite unbothered in alleging that she went through such an experience as the charges against the nine Negro lads imply.[20]

The final witnesses for the first day were R.R. Bridges and Marvin Lynch, the two physicians who examined Price and Bates on the day of the alleged rape. Bridges testified that if two men had raped one woman, she would show significant physical signs of being assaulted, such as large scratches, blood, and bruising in the genital area. Neither girl displayed such signs. Price only had a few minor scratches on her left arm and small bruises on her hips. In fact, Bridges said that rather than being hysterical, as he assumed a rape victim would be, the girls spoke calmly while he examined them. However, he said both girls showed indications that they had engaged in sexual intercourse about the time of the incident and that it was possible a rape had occurred. This last statement handed the jury all it needed to find the pair guilty.

Lynch then stepped to the witness stand and supported what Bridges had stated. Roddy, who had asked only a few quick questions of Price instead of putting her through an intense cross-examination, had no rebuttal and sat mute at the defense table. As it was late afternoon when Lynch finished his testimony, Hawkins adjourned the trial for the day.

Spectators poured out of the courtroom to a town center congested with revelers in Scottsboro. Vendors hawked food and drinks, and a brass band played tunes such as "There'll Be a Hot Time in the Old Town Tonight" and "Dixie." Everyone assumed that Norris and Weems would be found guilty the next day, with the other seven following in fast order.

Day Two

Ruby Bates led off testimony on day two of the trial. Whereas Price had confidently testified on Monday, quickly answering every question and displaying little doubt about who attacked her, Bates gave contradictory testimony and appeared confused and uncomfortable, frequently hesitating before answering. She could not state who had raped her, the order in which they raped her, and said that fewer than ten black males had hopped into the gondola rather than the dozen that Price claimed. Her testimony led reporters covering the trial for major newspapers to describe her as a weak witness for the prosecution.

Ransdell interviewed Bates and discovered that Bates, rather than being angry against the nine blacks charged with the crime, was irritated at Price. Ransdell listened as Bates, whom she described as "a large, fresh, good-looking girl,"[21] talked, spitting snuff juice onto the floor and wiping her mouth with her sleeve.

> The only strong feeling that Ruby showed about the case was not directed against the Negroes. It was against Victoria Price that Ruby expressed deep and bitter resentment. For Victoria captured the show for herself and pushed Ruby into the background, causing people at the trial to say that Victoria was a quick clever girl, but Ruby was slow and stupid. It was easier for Victoria to talk than to breathe. Words came hard to Ruby.[22]

Roddy had an opportunity to exploit these differences between Price and Bates, to suggest the girls were lying about the attack, but he failed to do so. He asked a few harmless questions that provided little help to his clients, although he did place on record that neither girl had mentioned any assault to police when the train first pulled into Paint Rock.

Prosecutor Bailey brought five other witnesses to the stand. James Broadway, one of the men who had been deputized at Paint Rock, surprised Bailey by claiming Price had never made any accusations at the depot. On the other hand, local citizens asserted they had witnessed the assault. Luther Morris said that he was standing in the loft to his barn about 30 yards (27.4m) from the track when the train passed by and that he saw the black males attack the girls. After Morris's testimony, Bailey rested his case. The defense attorneys would now have their chance to convince the jury of their clients' innocence.

Ruby Bates

Born in 1915, Ruby Bates was quieter than her friend Victoria Price. While Price delivered quotable phrases to the press and in the courtroom, Bates usually kept a lower profile. Also a product of a poor Alabama childhood, Bates turned to the rails to travel about the countryside, in the process coming into contact with other individuals experiencing hard times.

Seventeen years old when she accused the black young men of raping her, Bates hated the publicity and notoriety that the trials brought to her and Price. After the trials ended, she moved to Washington State in 1940, married a man named Elmer Schut, and called herself Lucille in hopes of masking her true identity. She died in 1976, one week after her husband passed away.

Testifying on day two of the trial, Ruby Bates gave testimony contradicting that of Victoria Price, appearing confused and uncomfortable. But the defense attorneys failed to use her testimony to benefit the defendants.

The Defendants Speak

The young men took the stand, but instead of helping themselves, they confused matters with their contradictory testimony. Each had his story about what happened and who participated. With the specter of the execution chair facing them, the nine turned against each other in hopes of saving their skins but only worsened their predicament by appearing untrustworthy and self-serving. "I can remember sitting there in this hot little courtroom," said Norris, "knowing that I'd never see my mother or sisters or anybody who I care about again. We all were thinking like this, and yes, things were getting desperate."[23]

Six of the nine—Weems, Andy Wright, Willie Roberson, Ozie Powell, Montgomery, and Eugene Williams—swore they had never even seen any girls in the gondola and had certainly not committed rape, while each of the other three—Norris, Patterson, and Roy Wright—accused the other eight of rape and denied he himself had a part in it. According to one reporter covering the trial, Norris's blunt statement all but closed the case for the prosecution when he said, "They all raped her, everyone of them."[24]

Roy Wright later said that he made his condemnation of his eight companions only after being beaten by jail guards. The youngster hoped to avoid further beatings and saw this step as the only way to stay alive. He told a reporter for the *New York Times* that he was sitting in a chair before Hawkins listening to the girls testifying when a deputy sheriff next to him leaned over and quietly asked if he was going to help the prosecutor by testifying against the other eight. Wright refused, claiming he knew nothing of the incident. "Then the trial stopped awhile," Wright told the reporter, F. Raymond Daniell,

> and the deputy sheriff beckoned to me to come out into another room—the room back of the place where the judge was sitting—and I went. They whipped me and it seemed like they was going to kill me. All the time they kept saying, 'Now will you tell?' and finally it seemed like I couldn't stand no more and I said yes. Then I went back into the courtroom and they put me up on the chair in front of the judge and began asking a lot of questions, and I said I had seen Charlie Weems and Clarence Norris in the gondola car with the white girls."[25]

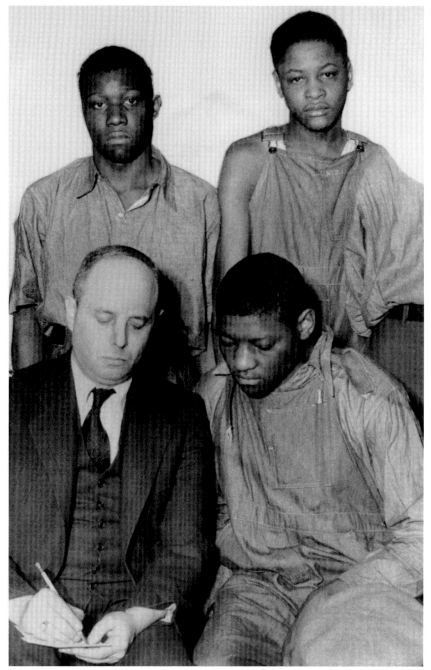

When testifying in their defense, Haywood Patterson (top left), Clarence Norris (top right), and Roy Wright (bottom right) each accused the other eight defendants of the rapes. Wright later said his actions were due to being beaten by the sheriff's deputies.

During a break, Roddy approached Bailey with a deal—the nine would plead guilty in exchange for life in prison instead of the death penalty. Bailey, who believed the evidence had gone his way—one newspaper editorial described Bailey's case as "so conclusive as to be almost perfect"[26]—and that the jury would most likely return with a guilty verdict and recommend execution, declined.

When the court reconvened, Roddy, convinced he could do no more, rested his case. Neither Roddy nor Moody presented a closing argument to the jury. In closing arguments lawyers summarize the facts of the case that help show the accused's innocence or guilt. After Bailey delivered his closing argument, in which he asked for the death penalty for Norris and Weems, Hawkins instructed the jury on their duties. He explained the charges, what the jury should look for, and, if they found the men guilty, what punishments they could attach.

Haywood Patterson's Trial

As the jury for the Weems-Norris trial left the courtroom to consider the evidence and arrive at a verdict, the jury for the second trial—that of Patterson—entered. Most observers expected a similar outcome for Patterson, and the lawyers had begun their opening statements when, two hours into Patterson's trial, the first jury notified Hawkins it had already reached a verdict.

Hawkins halted Patterson's trial and asked the jury to leave the courtroom and wait in a nearby room. When the twelve white males had departed, Hawkins brought in the Weems-Norris jury, whose foreman announced that it had found both men guilty and decided upon the death sentence for both.

A raucous outburst rose from the crowded courtroom as spectators yelled and whistled. Some rushed outside to deliver the news to the crowd of fifteen hundred people, who erupted in wild cheering and applause as the brass band began playing triumphant marches.

Roddy objected to the spectacle. He claimed that the outbursts would only influence the second jury, which had certainly heard the commotion. How could it do anything but bring in a guilty verdict for Patterson after listening to their friends outside? Hawkins brought the second jury back in, asked the members if

Haywood Patterson took the stand in his own defense but gave confusing testimony. The jury found him guilty after deliberating for just two hours.

they had been swayed by the noise, and allowed the case to proceed when they answered they could deliver a fair verdict.

Patterson hurt his chances by giving confusing testimony. He said he had only watched the attack from atop the next train car along with the Wrights and Williams, but he spoke with such uncertainty that the jury could hardly believe his words. He then added that he had helped Orville Gilley back onto the gondola, which a man about to commit rape would never do, but the testimony only perplexed the jury more. Had he witnessed the attack from the next car, or had he been in the gondola? Roddy called four other witnesses to the stand to testify on his behalf, but courtroom reporters concluded they did little to improve Patterson's chances. Two hours after listening to all the witnesses and leaving to consider the charges, the jury returned with a guilty verdict. Because Hawkins administered a severe warning against any outbursts, as had happened with the first trial, the verdict was read to a silent courtroom.

"Within two hours the jury had come back with a conviction," Patterson wrote years later. "I was convicted in their minds before I went on trial. I had no lawyers, no witnesses for me." He added of the all-white jury, "All that spoke for me on that witness stand was my black skin—which didn't do so good."[27]

The Trials End

A pattern had occurred that would be played out two more times on Wednesday—a speedy trial followed by a quick guilty verdict. Next to be tried were Wright, Williams, Powell, Montgomery, and Roberson. For this third trial the two girls again testified, with Bates claiming six men had raped her. Roddy, however, countered that Roberson's syphilis made it highly unlikely he participated and prodded Bridges into agreeing that such an act would be quite painful for the defendant. On the witness stand, Montgomery claimed he was sitting in the rear of the gondola and was too blind to see much of anything, Williams said he was in a different car and did not even see either girl until the train reached Paint Rock, and all flatly denied having done anything to Price and Bates.

The third trial wrapped up, the jury left the courtroom to deliberate, and the final trial for the youngest accused, Roy Wright, started. Yet another jury heard similar testimony introduced by both prosecution and defense lawyers, but this time the state, cognizant of Wright's tender age, asked only for life in prison rather than the death penalty.

The four-day drama ended Thursday. The jury for the third trial, after another quick deliberation, found all five men guilty and assessed the death penalty. Only Roy Wright's jury differed. The jurors readily agreed that he was guilty, but seven members held out for the death sentence rather than agree to Bailey's request for life imprisonment. When that jury's foreman informed Hawkins that they were hopelessly deadlocked, Hawkins declared a mistrial and ordered a new trial for Roy Wright.

Reaction to the Verdicts

Reaction from reporters covering the trials was predictable, with the local press favoring the convictions and outside publications condemning the results. "If ever there was an excuse for taking the law into their own hands, surely this was one,"[28] printed the *Scottsboro Progressive Age*, which heralded local citizenry for showing admirable restraint in not doing so. The Huntsville *Daily Times* claimed each Negro had been given his day in court, and the *Fairhope Courier* wrote on April 9 that the electric chair at Kilby Prison would soon be very busy.

Ransdell, covering the trials for the American Civil Liberties Union, assessed matters differently and reflected the viewpoint held by much of the nation outside the South.

> In three days' time, eight Negro boys all under 21, four of them under 18 and two of them sixteen or under, were hurried through trials which conformed only in outward appearance to the letter of the law. Given no chance even to communicate with their parents and without even as much as the sight of one friendly face, these eight boys, little more than children, surrounded entirely by white hatred and blind venomous prejudice, were sentenced to be killed in the electric chair at the earliest possible moment permitted by law. It is no exaggeration certainly to call this a legal lynching.[29]

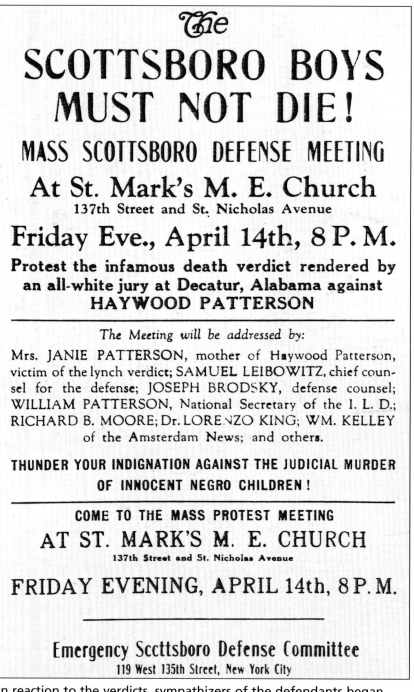

In reaction to the verdicts, sympathizers of the defendants began organizing and raising funds to appeal the all-white jury's convictions of the Scottsboro Boys.

Before Hawkins could issue his sentences—he had the power to affirm or to overturn the juries' verdicts—he and Benjamin Miller received similar telegrams sent by the International Labor Defense (ILD) of the American Communist Party. Calling the trials a miscarriage of justice in which the nine were framed for doing something they had not done, the ILD sought fair treatment for the accused. The ILD telegram read: "We demand stay of execution and opportunity to investigate and prepare for new trial or appeal. We demand right for our attorney to interview defendants and to obtain formal approval of defense counsel. And, above all, we demand absolute safety for the defendants against lynching."[30]

Both Hawkins and Miller objected to what they considered outside interference from people who neither lived in the South nor understood its ways. Even Roddy, the defense attorney, joined in condemning this intrusion into what was a local issue. Each provided a statement for the *New York Times*. "They were given every opportunity to provide themselves with counsel," Hawkins fired back, "and I appointed able members of the Jackson County bar to represent them. More than 1,000 members of the Alabama National Guard have been stationed here to protect them."[31] Bailey added, "It is hardly the time for any New York defense to claim the Negroes are being railroaded. There has been no violence of any nature and no talk of lynching."[32] Roddy agreed with Hawkins and Bailey that the nine had been treated fairly. "I do not see how any one can say that we are not striving to see that the defendants are getting the fairest trial."[33]

Late in the Afternoon of April 9 Hawkins pronounced sentences for the eight men found guilty. The crowded courtroom fell silent as Hawkins, moved to tears as he issued the death sentence for the first time in his career, stated that "it is the judgment of the court and the sentence of the law that the defendants be sentenced to death by electrocution at Kilby Prison in the city of Montgomery, Montgomery County, Alabama, on Friday the 10th day of July, 1931."[34] Hawkins asked each of the eight whether they had anything to say, but each declined.

"Stoically calm, eight negroes today were sentenced to die in the electric chair at Kilby Prison on Friday, July 10, for an attack on two young Huntsville girls," wrote the *Montgomery Advertiser*.

The article stated that "While the negroes showed no emotion, Judge Hawkins's eyes were wet with tears as one after the other he pronounced the sentence. It was the first time the jurist had pronounced a death sentence in his five years on the bench."[35]

The trials had barely ended before a new controversy tossed the proceedings into disarray. New lawyers and new organizations came to town, and nothing was the same.

Chapter Three

Legal Battles

Judge Alfred E. Hawkins had told Stephen R. Roddy that while he did not think the eight men deserved the death penalty, the interference by a Communist organization had so angered citizens in the South that it was a factor in his decision to go along with the juries. Southerners at the time preferred to handle matters on their own, but the fates of the nine men were about to be taken out of their hands.

Help for the Accused

The night after being sentenced the eight condemned prisoners, figuring they had nothing to lose if they tried to escape, rioted in the Gadsden jail. They beat on the cell bars, ripped their bedding, shouted for better food, and cursed the guards, who rushed in with clubs drawn and beat and kicked the men. Sheriff T.L. Griffin, whose family lived in the lower floor of the jail, removed them to a safer location in case the eight broke free, but in short order the guards had subdued the prisoners and placed them in irons.

Seeing no hope, two of the men vented their frustrations in letters to parents. "They didn't give me a fair trial," said Andy Wright in a letter to his mother written by Olen Montgomery.

"They are going to kill us for nothing. You know I would not do a thing like that."[36]

Haywood Patterson was more emotional in his letter home, telling his parents "that your poor son is going to die for nothing" and begging them to "do all you can to save me from being put to death for nothing. Mother, do what you can to save your son. We did not get a fair trial," he continued, "and you try to have it moved somewhere else if we get a new trial. Do you all try to come down here and try to get me a new trial or I will be put to death on July 10." He ended what had to be a heart-wrenching letter for his parents to read by claiming, "I am in jail for something I did not do. You know that it hurt me to my heart."[37]

Thousands of people nationwide marched to condemn the verdicts and to call for a new, fair trial.

A few rays of sunshine broke through the hopelessness. Thousands of people throughout the nation rallied to their defense, sending so many telegrams and letters to Alabama officials that Benjamin Miller refused to accept them. "Is condemning eight teen-agers to death on the testimony of two white prostitutes your idea of 'enlightened' Alabama justice?,"[38] one New York college student wrote Hawkins on April 13, 1931. People, including famed scientist Albert Einstein and noted science fiction writer H.G. Wells, signed petitions asking for the release of the Scottsboro Nine, and protesters staged rallies in many northern cities, Cuba, and throughout Europe.

The ILD Enters the Fight

As early as April 2 the *Daily Worker*, the newspaper for the American Communist Party, accused southern officials of incarcerating the Scottsboro Nine not because of any crime they committed but because those entrenched in power hoped to disrupt the unity emerging throughout the South between black and white workers. Backed by big-business owners, the paper added, Alabama wanted to frame the nine blacks.

The American Communist Party saw an opportunity in the Great Depression not only to rally unemployed workers against wealthy industrialists but also make gains among a group that had long languished on the outside—blacks. The party stated that American capitalists—the owners of large business firms—were responsible for workers' current troubles by retaining all the profits instead of sharing the wealth with their laborers. The party organized the International Labor Defense (ILD) to help those accused of crimes, offered free legal advice, and organized protests on their behalf. They saw in this case a golden opportunity to promote their causes.

On April 20 Joseph R. Brodsky and Allan Taub, two lawyers hired by the ILD, visited the prisoners to offer their help. To the astonishment of the Scottsboro Nine, who were unaccustomed to friendly gestures from whites, these lawyers brought candy and soda and said they could raise money on their behalf from workers around the world. They promised to mount a spirited effort to free them of the charge and return them to their families. The nine agreed, with Andy Wright affixing his signature and the others marking with an X a document handing the case over to the ILD lawyers. Brodsky and Taub hired a local attorney, George W. Chamlee Jr., to assist them with the customs of Alabama courts and the ways of the state's legal system. They hoped that Chamlee, the grandson of a prominent Confederate veteran who fought for the South in the Civil War, would also bring respectability and gain acceptance for the ILD from southerners.

Three days later Roddy, caught flat-footed by the unexpected move, convinced the nine that associating with a team of Communist-supported lawyers would harm their chances. He explained that

The Communist View

From the start, the American Communist Party took an active role in coming to the aid of the nine Scottsboro Boys. While they organized mass protests and sent legal help supposedly to gain freedom for the accused, they also wanted to draw members to its cause and unite workers in what the party saw as a worldwide fight against big businesses.

A 1932 pamphlet, *They Shall Not Die! The Story of Scottsboro in Pictures*, published by a Communist-affiliated group, expresses the views of the party in its struggle to gain freedom for the nine as well as what it saw as justice for workers in the country.

> The bosses had thought that no one would care about the fate of nine jobless 'n******.' And now were heard the voices of millions, roaring protest.

> Always the bosses had tried to divide the white workers from the Negroes—and here were white workers, taking their places in the very forefront of the struggle for the freedom of nine black boys!

> Scottsboro stands today as a symbol of the national oppression of the Negroes, of the bosses' oppression of the whole working-class. The cause of the nine Scottsboro boys is the cause of all the workers, Negro and white.

League of Struggle for Negro Rights. *They Shall Not Die! The Story of Scottsboro in Pictures*. New York: Workers' Library, 1932, pp. 13–14. http://archive.lib.msu.edu/DMC/ AmRad/shall notdie.pdf.

From the very beginning, the Communist Party took an active role in aiding the Scottsboro Nine.

Communists wanted to overthrow the American system of government, that they followed orders from Communist leaders in the Soviet Union, and that their presence would antagonize southerners. The prisoners signed a document asking the ILD to step away and allow Roddy to continue as defense attorney.

Appeal to the Parents

Brodsky and Taub executed a deft move by going to the parents and gaining their support. They treated them with respect and explained what they could do for their sons. This impressed the parents, who were flattered that two white lawyers visited their homes, and they agreed to urge their sons to place their fates in

Haywood Patterson's mother Janie (pictured with Sam Leibowitz, center, and police escorts) arrives in New York City to rally support for the Scottsboro Nine. About the issue of being helped by Communists, she said that they were the only people who fought to save the boys.

Emotions Run High

───────────■───────────

Different events surrounding the trials indicated the high state of emotion that existed in Alabama. At a secret nighttime 1931 meeting at a rural Alabama church, several hundred blacks joined to discuss ways to improve their economic position in southern society. A Communist organizer told the crowd that the recent Scottsboro convictions were no better than "legal lynching" and suggested they unite to oppose them.

The meeting ended suddenly when Sheriff Kyle Young and his deputies arrived at the church to break up the assembly. Angry words followed, which led to gunshots ringing in the dark. Young and a deputy fell wounded, as did one of the blacks inside.

As other attendees fled the church, four wounded blacks remained behind. Deputies arrested them, burned the church to the ground, and with bloodhounds howling scoured the countryside for other blacks who had been at the gathering. They arrested sixty blacks, but the four wounded fugitives were never again seen. When asked about what had happened to the four who had been seized at the church, the town's police chief remarked, "They went out to chop stove wood and haven't returned yet." The rest of the blacks in the area were so frightened of what might happen to them that they moved to neighboring counties.

Time."Races: In Tallapoosa." July 27, 1931.

their hands. They signed a document stating that even though their sons were legal minors, the parents had never been consulted about selecting Roddy. Instead, they wanted the ILD in charge. Ada Wright, who had two sons in jail, later said the ILD had "been very honest from the beginning, being the only organization or individual that ever came to the parents and discussed the case with them, and asked their support."[39]

Janie Patterson wrote her son on April 24, "I don't want Roddy to have nothing to do with you," and added he was not to "let nobody turn you around from what Mama says." Haywood's father was stronger in his note, telling his son, "You will burn sure if you don't let them preachers alone and trust in the International Labor Defense to handle the case."[40]

Accompanied by Chamlee, Mrs. Wright, Mrs. Williams, and Mr. Patterson visited their sons in jail to persuade them to sign with the ILD. After a few moments of hugging and crying, the parents chatted with their sons and the others and convinced them to again work with the ILD.

The ILD wasted no time in gaining sympathizers and raising money throughout the nation by sending the parents to different American cities. Ada Wright and her daughter traveled through the Midwest and Northeast, Mamie Williams covered the South, Ida Norris appeared along the West Coast, and Viola Montgomery spoke to rallies in the Southwest.

The parents praised the ILD's efforts. "If it hadn't been for the ILD," declared Mamie Williams in North Carolina, "we mothers wouldn't have been able to see our boys, I guess, until judgment day."[41]

Janie Patterson addressed a large rally in New York City on April 24. She bluntly addressed the issue of being helped by Communists, also called Reds after the color of their flag in the Soviet Union, by proclaiming, "I don't care whether they are Reds, Greens or Blues. They are the only ones who put up a fight to save these boys and I am with them to the end."[42]

The NAACP Enters

The National Association for the Advancement of Colored People (NAACP), the nation's oldest and most respected civil rights organization, muddied the waters by trying to talk the parents into abandoning the ILD and going with them. The NAACP had at first been reluctant to become involved until they were convinced the nine men had not raped the girls. Their leaders believed they could not risk their organization's reputation by defending rapists and waited until they were certain the men were being framed. However, the delay allowed the ILD to make its case to the parents and prisoners.

Leaders from the NAACP argued that the ILD rallies and speeches angered southerners and that a quieter approach would work better. They claimed that the boys would never receive a fair trial as long as they were associated with Communists, and contended that the Communists were only involved in the case to gain the party more members.

The ILD condemned the NAACP as an overly cautious group that would do nothing to irritate the white establishment. Whereas the NAACP viewed the parents as uneducated, ill-informed individuals, the ILD cleverly treated them with respect at every step in the process. Realizing that they were being outmaneuvered, the NAACP turned to the country's most acclaimed defense attorney, Clarence Darrow, who built a reputation as a battler for the underdog in hundreds of cases. Darrow traveled to Alabama to meet with the prisoners.

The debate raged into the summer of 1931. Prison guards warned the accused that if they remained with the Communists, they would die for certain, while a stream of lawyers and parents poured in and out of the jail, each bringing their own arguments. "I didn't know nothing about the ILD or the NAACP," says Clarence Norris. "I wanted all the help I could get from anybody." When both organizations stated they would not handle the defense unless the opposing organization was out, Norris added, "I never did understand why they couldn't work together, since they all said they wanted to see us free."[43]

By late May the nine prisoners had split. The Wright brothers, Patterson, Eugene Williams, and Montgomery sided with the ILD; Ozie Powell, Charlie Weems, and Norris favored the NAACP; while Willie Roberson fluctuated back and forth. As the dispute over legal representation took so much time, on June 22, 1931, Hawkins set aside the execution date for the eight condemned men.

Southern Objections

Most people in the South detested what they considered interference from outside sources. They believed that unless one was born in the South, a person could not grasp the complexities of the racial issues in the region and should thus stay out of what was not their concern.

"To Hell with 'em we say," editorialized the Dothan *Wiregrass Journal* on July 31, 1931. "We've not asked for their advice. Don't need it and feel that we are entirely capable of handling our own affairs without outside interference."[44]

Southerners countered that rather than being truly interested in the black defendants' innocence or guilt, the Communists only wanted to cause trouble in the region, and the NAACP saw the nine as pawns in the larger struggle for racial equality throughout the country. Some argued that while critics of the South contended that Alabama wanted to execute the eight simply because they were black, those same critics labored to save them for the same reason, regardless of whether they were innocent or guilty.

"It is inconceivable to the authors that anyone who has followed the coverage of the Scottsboro case," penned one southern writer covering the events, "as it has been reported by the more reliable press associations of the country, can fail to realize that the Communist party has seized upon this case for only one reason—to stir up race antagonism in the Black Belt of the South."[45]

Signs warned outsiders that the Ku Klux Klan (KKK), a Southern organization opposing attempts to grant blacks any rights, would resort to violence if necessary to protect southern customs, and lawyers for the ILD received threats against their lives unless they left town. "There was no intimidation of the court and the jury from Jackson County people," stated Grover Hall, the editor of the *Montgomery Advertiser*. "The only attempt at intimidation came from New York, where [author Theodore] Dreiser's idiotic committee is headquartered. That committee sent threatening telegrams to the judge. It was a fair and orderly procedure, from beginning to end, and under the laws of this State, the decision is just."[46]

In the face of the hostility, southerners offered each other support for what was occurring in the Scottsboro case. One Alabama citizen wrote to Miller that the "God fearing people of the South truly hope no threat or demand from dirty Yankees or damn communists from the North and throughout the world will sway you either way in the death sentence of the [eight] negroes for assaulting white girls."[47]

Another Alabama citizen told a friend from the North, "I might have been for acquittin' them at the first trial, but now after all this stink's been raised, we've got to hang 'em,"[48] while an elderly woman told Hollace Ransdell that she hoped the nine blacks were lynched.

The Nine Select the ILD

The ILD and NAACP continued their attempts to gain control of the case until late December 1931, when the nine men informed the NAACP that if it wished to continue working on their behalf, it would have to cooperate with the ILD. Darrow replied that he would sever his ties with the NAACP if Brodsky and Chamlee cut theirs with the ILD, but knowing they had the support of the parents the ILD held firm. Seeing little hope in continuing without Communist interference, Darrow withdrew from the case. He gave as his reason for leaving that "the case was controlled by the Communist party, who cared far less for the safety and well-being of those poor Negro boys than the exploitation of their own cause. If I could not be free and completely independent, without political ties, I would have none of it."[49]

The NAACP, surprised that the nine defendants would spurn the esteemed civil rights organization, withdrew with Darrow. Walter White, executive secretary of the NAACP, asked Andy Wright why they selected a Communist organization over a group that had done so much for equal rights in the United States. His answer was clear and blunt. "Mr. White, if you can't trust your mother, who can you trust?"[50]

Norris added the other significant reason when he explained that the issue boiled down to which group showed more interest in their problems. "Most of us refused to accept the NAACP because they weren't there for us in the beginning of the case." Norris later wrote about the ILD, "My mind will never lead me to drop this organization. They have did to greater work in this fight to see that I get justice for a crime I am absolutely innocent of," and that, "if it wasn't for that communist organization trying to save our lives, we would have went to the chair on the 10th of July 1931."[51]

To Alabama's Supreme Court

On June 22, 1931, the execution dates were stayed, or placed on hold, pending an appeal of the cases to the Alabama Supreme Court. The ILD knew it had little chance of succeeding, but it was a necessary first step in taking it to the U.S. Supreme Court in Washington, D.C., where the ILD expected a more favorable reception.

Chamlee's welcome at the Alabama Supreme Court on January 21, 1932, left no doubt about the outcome. With each judge staring coldly at the ILD lawyer, Chief Justice John C. Anderson remarked that the flood of letters the Court had received from around the country on behalf of the defendants, some containing death threats, was not only improper but sent in an attempt to sway the judges. Though Chamlee claimed that the ILD had nothing to do with the torrent of mail, the judges appeared unconvinced by his statement. Chamlee added that the nine had been denied the right to an adequate defense by the speed with which they were brought to trial and that they had not had a chance to meet with counsel until the first day of trial.

Brodsky followed. He stated that a jury of their peers had not judged the defendants as the U.S. Constitution requires, as the

Attorneys George W. Chamlee (center) and Joseph R. Brodsky (right, pictured with Sam Leibowitz) argued before the Alabama Supreme Court that the Scottsboro Nine did not, for many reasons, get fair trials. The court ruled in favor of the prosecution but did overturn Eugene Williams's conviction because he was a juvenile.

juries were solely comprised of white males. He asserted that the crowds surrounding the court, the celebration after hearing the first verdict, the presence of the National Guard, and the biased newspaper coverage negatively affected the juries, and that Roy Wright should have been tried in juvenile court.

The Alabama attorney general, Thomas G. Knight Jr., presented the prosecution's side the next day. Chamlee and Brodsky knew he would receive a warmer greeting from the Alabama judges, especially as his father, Thomas Sr., happened to be one of the judges listening to his arguments. Knight presented a simple argument, stating that the crowd had not gathered to threaten or influence anyone but only to protect the rights of white women everywhere.

Two months later, on March 24, 1932, the Alabama Supreme Court ruled in favor of the prosecution by upholding all but one of the convictions. The court ruled that Williams's youth required that he be tried as a juvenile and thus ordered a new trial, but it also ruled that the other men had received fair treatment. The judges stated that Hawkins had committed no error in denying the defense request for a change of venue and that the trials' speed was to be praised. "If there were more speed and less delay in the administration of the criminal laws of the land, life and property would be infinitely safer and greater respect would the criminally inclined have for the law."[52] To support its conclusion, the court referred to the aftermath of the 1901 assassination of President William McKinley, when the trial for the accused occurred within ten days and execution happened less than two months later.

The judges ruled that the presence of the National Guard helped maintain order, that news coverage was fair, that the crowd had gathered only for song and fun, and that Price's character should have nothing to do with the charges, as rape could occur to anyone, even a prostitute. The court set a new execution date of May 13. Only Anderson dissented. Chamlee announced that the ILD would immediately appeal the rulings to the U.S. Supreme Court.

Anderson, a brilliant jurist who normally persuaded the other judges to follow his lead, found himself in the minority. He argued that the speed of the trials hurt the defendants, as the trials were held when emotions were at a peak, that the National Guard had influenced the juries, and that the defense attorneys proved unreliable. He asserted that the fact that each jury handed out the death sentence to each defendant, despite their differences in ages and situations, proved they had been influenced by outside events. Anderson concluded that the men had thus been denied a fair and impartial trial as guaranteed by the Bill of Rights and were entitled to new trials.

Reaction was predictable. Most newspapers and politicians in the South supported the judges, while condemnation poured in from elsewhere. Roger Baldwin, the director of the American Civil Liberties Union, said, "The Alabama Supreme Court runs true to Southern form in upholding the death verdict in the Scottsboro case. Considering the general attitude in the South toward any rape case, however disputed the facts, it was hardly to be expected that a new trial would be ordered."[53]

To the U.S. Supreme Court

The ILD's real purpose was to get the case to the U.S. Supreme Court, where they counted on receiving a fairer reception. The May 13 execution date was set aside to grant time for defense attorneys to take the case to the nation's highest court. To present their case before the judges in Washington, D.C., the ILD hired a constitutional expert, attorney Walter Pollack. On October 10, 1932, Pollack argued that the crowds had influenced the trials and that the defendants were so young and confused that they did not grasp the gravity of their situation nor demand adequate counsel. Pollack pointed to unfair newspaper coverage as a factor in heightening the emotions surrounding the case, and claimed that Hawkins erred in not allowing the case to be heard elsewhere.

Knight disagreed with Pollack. He pointed to the presence of the National Guard as proof that the state of Alabama had taken every step to protect the defendants, that Roddy and Moody had provided good counsel, and that the friendly crowds exerted no influence over anyone.

The Supreme Court announced its decision on November 7. Justice George Sutherland, speaking for the court, addressed a quiet room. Normally one of the most conservative voices on the court and someone who opposed federal intervention into state affairs, Sutherland in *Powell* v. *Alabama* pronounced that the

Scottsboro Boys had been denied the right to adequate counsel, that they had been unable to select their own lawyers, and that they had not even been able to meet with a lawyer until the morning of the first trial, all of which violated their rights under the Fourteenth Amendment to the Constitution.

Sutherland emphasized that as the Constitution guarantees an accused a trial by one's peers, by his equals, rights were further denied in the Scottsboro cases, where only white males served on juries. Sutherland referred to the influence exerted by the crowds and said, "It is perfectly apparent that the proceedings from beginning to end took place in an atmosphere of tense, hostile and excited public sentiment."[54] Sutherland then announced that the Supreme Court had reversed the guilty verdicts and was ordering new trials.

Demonstrators clash in front of the U.S. Supreme Court during the hearing of *Powell v. Alabama*. The Court reversed the convictions and ordered new trials.

Reaction

Reaction came fast. The *New York Times* praised the decision in *Powell* v. *Alabama* as reaffirming the rights of everyone and answering the communist charges that the government and courts only existed for the benefit of the wealthy and powerful. "It is not often that we see the issue of justice to the lowliest, and possibly most unworthy, so clearly appearing in an important judicial decision," the newspaper stated in an editorial after the announcement. "It ought to abate the rancor of extreme radicals, while confirming the faith of the American people in the soundness of their institutions and especially in the integrity of their courts."[55]

The Alabama Ku Klux Klan reacted to the Supreme Court's ruling in *Powell v. Alabama* by ramping up terrorist activities against the black community, which included threats and intimidation.

Southerners condemned the decision as an intrusion of the Supreme Court into what was a state matter, although the *Birmingham News* thought that another trial would give the state a chance to show that it could be more than fair. The Alabama Ku Klux Klan, on the other hand, dropped pamphlets from a Birmingham building on two thousand blacks demonstrating below, warning, "Negroes of Birmingham, the Ku Klux Klan is watching you. Tell the Communists to get out of town. They mean only trouble for you, for Alabama is a good place for good Negroes and a bad place for Negroes who believe in racial equality."[56]

The ILD credited itself for the Supreme Court decision, claiming that the court was forced by "the powerful mass protest, embracing millions of workers throughout the world at the initiative of the Communist Party and the International Labor Defense."[57] Although the ILD's expression showed their interests lay more in the worldwide Communist movement than in justice for nine black southerners, the organization had at least gained the accused another trial.

The men in jail certainly appreciated their efforts. "Since the Supreme Court have granted we boys a new trial," Montgomery wrote in a thank you letter to the ILD on November 8, 1932, "I thank it is my rite to express thanks and appreciation to the whole party for their care." He added "I my self feels like I have been born again from the worrying."[58] His companion, Patterson, felt the ruling proved that Alabama authorities had mistreated them. "They said that showed we were gypped out of a defense."[59]

With its decision in *Powell* v. *Alabama* the Supreme Court reaffirmed a crucial notion for the nation's citizens—that anyone accused of a crime, especially one in which the death penalty may be involved, has the right to speedy and adequate counsel under the Fourteenth Amendment. This ruling would become even more important twenty years later, when the civil rights movement gained momentum, but in 1932 it handed the accused new life.

Unfortunately, while lawyers and judges spent months pondering their fates, much of that new life had been spent in horrible conditions.

Chapter Four

A Prisoner's World

In the meantime, while lawyers from the International Labor Defense (ILD) and Alabama state officials gathered evidence and the Supreme Court issued its rulings, as weeks stretched into months and the months into years, the nine languished in miserable jail conditions. At times they became the forgotten ones, unseen and unheard from in their deplorable cells and living a bleak existence for crimes they did not commit while other people decided their fates.

Living in Squalor

Alabama moved the nine from prison to prison while the trials unfolded. They spent their first months in Kilby Prison near Montgomery, Alabama, behind concrete walls topped with barbed wire and armed guards. Alabama took pride in Kilby, at eight years old it was its newest prison facility and one offering a dairy farm, cotton mill, slaughterhouse, and hospital.

Behind the walls, however, the miserable conditions told another story. The cells were little bigger than glorified closets—five paces from front to back and so narrow a man could stand in the middle and touch both sides with outstretched arms. Besides the two double-decker bunks for sleeping, the cells offered only a wash basin, a toilet, and one small window to the rear. A dark screen covered the cell door, blocking the view toward the aisle separating the two rows of cells. The cell windows on one side of the row looked out at another building, but the more fortunate prisoners who occupied the other row at least enjoyed a view of the prison yard and baseball field.

The food was hardly sufficient to sustain a growing man. Clarence Norris described the inadequate fare as "beans, greens, and no meat to be seen,"[60] and Ozie Powell took up most of a December 1932 letter to his mother asking her to bring food the

The Scottsboro defendants meet with their lawyers at the Decatur jail. Although the state had condemned the facility for housing white prisoners, the state felt it was good enough for black prisoners.

next time she visited him. He wrote that he would be thrilled if she could bring

> 1 coconut, 2 nice cakes, chocolate and coconut, 1 pound mixed nuts, 1 doz. Apples, 1 doz. Oranges, 1 doz. bananas and candy, 3 blocks of grape chewing gum, 2 pairs of socks and some cheese and some fried rabbit and sausage and some fried potato pies and some sauce meat and some Rex-all tooth paste and some stamps envelopes and tablet.[61]

In March 1933 eight of the nine were transferred to the jail in Decatur, Alabama, where the second round of new trials was being held. As hideous as Kilby Prison was, Decatur, standing near Birmingham, made it look like a vacation resort. The state of Alabama had condemned the dilapidated structure two years earlier as unfit for white prisoners but still used it to house black prisoners. Authorities crammed the men into one cell, which reeked of urine and dead animals. Roaches and large rats ran freely about the grounds. After meeting with the prisoners, a visitor described them as "terrified, bewildered," inhabiting their filthy cell like "scared little mice, caught in a trap."[62]

"The Decatur jail was a hellhole," writes Norris of his home for ten months.

> It was filthy, dust everywhere, big holes were in the floors and walls, plaster fell down around our heads, the stink was sickening and the rats the size of rabbits had the run of the place. But the bedbugs! There were millions of them, large as grains of rice. They crawled all over us at night and sleep was hard to come by. The bloodsuckers almost drained us dry.[63]

Making conditions worse was the thought that the young men endured the squalor and rats even though they heatedly argued they were innocent of the crime for which they were accused. Whether in Decatur or some other run-down structure, each morning they awakened to another twenty-four hours of fear, appalling living conditions, inadequate food and medical treatment, all for crimes they had not committed. Compounding their dilemma was that they had no idea how long their nightmare behind bars would last. They would remain incarcerated for the duration of the trials, which would take years at least, and then, if fortunate enough to avoid the electric chair, most likely spend the rest of their lives in jail. The ordeal was enough to test the endurance of the sanest of men.

Guards typically awakened them around 5:30 every morning. After a simple breakfast, the accused had little to do but wait alone with their thoughts. Other prisoners enjoyed exercise periods, but prison authorities often denied that privilege to the Scottsboro defendants, who spent the day staring at the walls or mumbling to each other. The nights offered little relief from their daytime horror. Instead of falling into a deep slumber and forgetting the day's terrors, the men rarely enjoyed a decent sleep as guards either walked through each hour and shined flashlights in their faces or left the jail lights on all night long.

The Death Chair

The guards at every institution added to their misery. Norris says that of the many difficulties he endured, "the hardest thing I had to deal with on a day-to-day basis at Kilby, both mentally and physically, were the sadistic guards. Man, they would beat you for the slightest thing."[64] The guards called them either n***** or boy, never by their given names. The nine became accustomed to four guards entering a cell, stretching one of the accused facedown on the floor and, while two guards sat on the legs and another on the shoulders, the fourth would wield a thick leather strap and beat the man on the back and buttocks with such ferocity the man could not sit down for days. A guard by the name of L.J. Burns targeted Haywood Patterson and Norris for his abuse, yanking them from their cells to punish them on several occasions. Alabama state law allowed the guards to take such actions when necessary, as long as the punishment was recorded in the prison's log, but many beatings went unrecorded.

Not every guard tormented the nine. One man at the Decatur jail smuggled whiskey and cigarettes into the prison for the defendants because he thought the men were being mistreated. As a Christian, the guard did not believe in abusing his charges and hoped to ease their predicaments by doing whatever he could. The guard's compassion surprised the captives, who began to realize that not everyone in the South was out to kill them.

The Ku Klux Klan

Begun in 1865 in the South in the aftermath of the Civil War, the Ku Klux Klan adopted violence and other measures to prevent the recently freed slaves from having equal rights and to maintain white supremacy. To protect their identities from federal authorities, Klan members dressed in robes and sheets and donned pointed white hoods. The Klan burned houses and schools, murdered people attempting to exercise their new-found rights, and spread fear among black Americans residing in the South.

In the 1920s the Klan expanded its targets to include immigrants, Jews, and Catholics. It gained new membership, increasing its numbers to almost 5 million, and turned to politics to elect public officials sympathetic to their views. The organization began to decline due to bitter divisions among its leadership and because much of the nation wearied of its reliance on violence and intimidation. By the end of World War II (1941–1945) the Klan had shrunk in significance. Though it experienced a small rebirth during the civil rights era of the 1950s and 1960s, the Klan today is a shadow of its glory years, having an estimated six thousand members.

The Ku Klux Klan marches in Washington, D.C., in 1925. At its peak, the Klan had over 5 million members.

However, misery overshadowed kindliness, and if any of the prisoners doubted the state's plans for them, the sight of other condemned men walking to the electric chair that rested in a room at the end of the hallway was a constant reminder. Known as "the death house," Kilby used an electric chair nicknamed the "Yellow Mama" to carry out the death sentences. During their incarceration the prisoners witnessed ten condemned men, all black, pass by their cells at midnight to the death chamber, many crying for their mothers as they walked toward the chair. The odor of burning flesh sometimes filtered into their cells after the executions, and guards used the executions to taunt the nine Scottsboro Boys about what awaited them.

The death of Will Stokes, who murdered a person with an ax, left an indelible impression on Patterson, who said later, "If I live to be a hundred I will never forget that day." Patterson and his companions halted talking when the moment arrived. "When they turned on the juice for Stokes we could hear the z-z-z-z-z-z of the electric current outside in the death row. The buzz went several times. After the juice was squeezed into him a guard came out and gave us a report. 'Stokes died hard. They stuck a needle through his head to make sure.'" Patterson, who faced a similar fate, adds, "I sweated my clothes wet."[65] Norris heard every word and sound as if he were in the chamber with Stokes. He claimed that afterward he was so sick from the ordeal that he could not sleep or eat for days.

Effects on Family

The burden of being separated from the outside world and suffering for a crime they had not committed was almost too much to bear. "At times I believe I am going insane,"[66] Roy Wright told friends. In a letter to George Maurer, an ILD official, Wright confided, "You know Mr. Maurer that at times it is really hard for me to get myself together in this place. Oh, to think what I am charged with. If there is a god as they say he knows I am not guilty of such hideous crime." He added, "You know I am idle in here and I think the whole thing over and over. To think there is people so unjust that they put things on people they don't know anything about. Well, nevertheless the good lord don't like ugly things so I'll trust in him for those that try to punish me for a deed I didn't commit."[67]

Norris lost weight because, with all the time on his hands and nothing to do with it, he spent his days worrying about what would happen to him. Patterson turned to new interests, such as learning how to write, to keep from going crazy. In December 1931 he surprised his mother by writing her a Christmas letter. All six of the men who could not read before going to jail learned how to do so during their months in prison.

No longer able to see family at will, the nine turned to corresponding with their parents, to whom they confided their hopes and fears. "While in my cell, lonely and thinking of you," Roy Wright wrote his mother on June 19, 1931, "I am trying by some means to write you a few words. I would like for you to come down here Thursday. I feel like I can eat some of your cooking Mom."[68] Olen Montgomery's lack of proper spelling did not detract from his ability to express his emotions, as he showed in a 1931 letter to George Chamlee: "i am in here for something i know i did not do my pore mother has no one to help hur to make a living."[69] Patterson said that one aspect bothered him above the rest—the pain his mother felt. "I had seen the main street of many a city and always looked for a decent job. Always I had in mind the dream I would bring home some money for my parents, help them out. Then one day they read the newspapers, and now Mother visited me in the death row."[70]

Help from Unexpected Places

Rays of sunshine filtered through the darkness. Strangers from around the nation, enraged about what happened to the men, mailed encouragement, candy, and money to the nine. Most of the accused were perplexed by the gifts, as white people had never before treated them with kindness, but they were happy to accept anything that eased their lives.

A handful of guards treated them with compassion, with a few even willing, for a price, to obtain food, clothes, and other items from outside prison. On occasion Norris was able to pay the prison cook to prepare his favorite meals, such as ham and eggs or steak.

The instances of decency boosted their morale, but they could not overshadow the atrocious conditions they endured day after day. A wholesome meal or new pair of pants paled in comparison to the continuous abuse they endured. Norris said that while he

Haywood Patterson (right, with attorney Joseph R. Brodsky) said in jail that the thought of the pain that his mother had endured during the ordeal made him very emotional. All the defendants were worried about the trial's effects on their families.

enjoyed the mail and the occasional kind word from a guard, he much preferred being on the outside looking in rather than the other way around.

The frustrations sometimes provoked clashes with authorities and even once among the nine. Roy and Andy Wright stabbed Patterson in the side, inflicting a wound requiring two stitches, because they found him so difficult and arrogant. On April 27, 1933, the prisoners stood on tables and chairs in their day cell—they were sometimes placed in a different cell during the day along with other inmates—and yelled at the guards to protest poor prison treatment in the Jefferson County jail. Sheriff James F. Hawkins ordered them confined with only bread and water until they stopped. After twenty hours, realizing the futility of their action, they relented and returned peacefully to their cells.

Preparation for More Trials

New lawyers for both sides and a different judge changed the circumstances for Patterson's second trial. Among them was one of the nation's top defense attorneys and a local judge who brought fairness and wisdom into a heated situation.

William L. Patterson, the executive secretary of the ILD, realized they needed the best lawyers available if they were to have any chance in the second round of trials. Clarence Darrow was generally recognized as the premier criminal attorney, but he had already dropped his connections with the case, so Secretary Patterson looked to New York lawyer Samuel S. Leibowitz, a man who had recorded seventy-seven acquittals and one hung jury—the twelve could not agree on a decision—in seventy-eight murder trials. A powerful presence in the courtroom, Leibowitz claimed his success came not because he was great but because he so thoroughly prepared for his cases.

Leibowitz had followed the case through the newspapers and was appalled at how poorly the defense lawyers had performed. In January 1933 he received a letter from Secretary Patterson asking for his services. The letter explained that the atmosphere surrounding the first trials—the speed with which they were held, the lynch mobs, machine guns, the soldiers that were present each day, and the band playing for the crowds—all hurt the defendants.

Twelve million Negroes in the United States have come to look upon Scottsboro as symbolizing their struggle for the right to live as human beings and the right to enjoy those privileges guaranteed by our constitution which unfortunately up to the present have remained, so far as these Negroes are concerned, mere paper rights.[71]

Secretary Patterson explained that he had no money to offer and that Leibowitz would have to pick up any costs, but he dangled a powerful inducement he hoped would prod the lawyer to accept.

We do have this to offer you: An opportunity to give your best in a cause which for its humanitarian appeal has never been equaled in the annals of American jurisprudence. You will not only be representing nine innocent boys, you will be representing a nation of twelve millions of oppressed people struggling against dehumanizing inequalities.[72]

The letter also said that Leibowitz would not have to agree with the views of the ILD should he take the case.

After receiving the letter Leibowitz investigated the ILD. While he detested their association with communism, he was impressed with their passion for the case and their ability to raise enough money to take the case to the U.S. Supreme Court. Leibowitz's friends tried to convince him that a Jewish lawyer from New York, arguing a case supported by Communists, would have no chance with a southern jury, but Leibowitz believed he could overcome any prejudices.

A few days after receiving Patterson's letter, Leibowitz replied that he would accept the case, not because he agreed with Communist beliefs but because the trial concerned "the basic rights of man." He said, "Some of my friends have advised me to take no part on this case. They fear that the defendants have been prejudged; that irrespective of the action of the appellate court, they are doomed because their skins are black. I cannot partake of that opinion." He added that all Americans share a respect for justice, and "I cannot believe that the people of Alabama will be false to their great heritage of honor, and to those brave and chivalrous generations of the past, in whose blood the history of

Samuel S. Leibowitz

Born in Romania in 1893, Samuel S. Leibowitz came to the United States with his parents in 1897. After his graduation from Cornell Law School in 1915, a lawyer friend suggested that Leibowitz change his last name to Lee to shed his immigrant status and better blend in with mainstream American society. Leibowitz, proud of his heritage, declined. He built a successful law practice and proved to be a gifted speaker and cross-examiner in court. As *Time* magazine put it in 1931, "A natural showman, daring, quick-witted, with expressive eyes, a mobile face, a wide-ranged resonant voice, the gift of oratory and an intuitive awareness of jury reactions, Lawyer Leibowitz's court successes came so unbelievably as to make him appear hypnotic."

Leibowitz was connected to two of the country's most sensational cases. Infamous Chicago gangster Al Capone hired Leibowitz in connection with three murders in Brooklyn's Adonis Club, and Leibowitz thought of defending Bruno Richard Hauptmann, who was accused of kidnapping and murdering the infant son of aviator Charles Lindbergh,

"if he will tell me the whole truth." After meeting with Hauptmann and concluding he could do nothing for the man, Leibowitz declined the case.

Time. "Law: Scottsboro Hero." August 2, 1937.

Samuel Leibowitz agreed to take the Scottsboro case because the trial concerned "the basic rights of man."

their State is written."[73] He informed Secretary Patterson that he would neither accept the ILD's money nor allow the ILD to pay his expenses. Joseph R. Brodsky and Chamlee would continue on the case as Leibowitz's assistants.

The Stage Is Set

Leibowitz arrived in Birmingham on March 13, 1933, to take over the defense. He thought he had good news in the form of a January 1933 letter supposedly written by Ruby Bates, in which she recanted her accusations and said she had not been raped. She claimed that the police forced her to lie about the nine men. She supposedly wrote that "those Negroes did not touch me or those white boys," and that "i was drunk at the time and did not know what i was doing i know it was wrong too let those Negroes die on account of me." The letter ended with Bates writing, "i wish those Negroes are not Burnt on account of me it is those white boys fault."[74]

Doubts arose as to the letter's validity when Hunstville police arrested a man named Miron Pearlman for drunkenness and found the note. Pearlman claimed that someone paid him to get Bates drunk and persuade her to write the letter, and Bates issued a statement denying any involvement. Though investigators found no evidence that the letter was fake, Leibowitz's plan to introduce the letter ended with Pearlman's arrest.

Hoping to eliminate some of the heated emotions that enveloped the trials at Scottsboro, the defense submitted a motion to Hawkins to move the case to another location. They wanted Birmingham, thinking that prejudices might be less a factor in a large city than they had been in rural Scottsboro. Hawkins agreed to the request for a change of venue but selected Decatur, Alabama, a small town of fifteen thousand residents 50 miles (80.46km) west of Scottsboro. The prosecution agreed to the motion, thinking that observers would accept it as evidence the state of Alabama wanted to ensure a fair trial for the accused. Less assured, Chamlee retorted that his clients would still have a need for military protection in Decatur.

A reporter for the *New York Times* agreed that prejudice in Alabama remained a factor, but he displayed prejudices of his own in writing of it:

As the hearing proceeded, the jurors, twelve bewhiskered mountaineers in the overalls and boots, uniform of the countryside, lounged in their chairs on a platform facing the bench and glared at the visitors from New York. Behind them sat twelve rows of lantern-jawed men of similar mien [appearance] and costume. There wasn't a Negro in the court house or near it while the case was being considered.[75]

Alabama attorney general Thomas E. Knight Jr. (left) and Assistant Attorney General Thomas Lawson would lead the prosecution in the second round of trials.

The reporter concluded that "Feeling is still very strong and there are many in Scottsboro who declare regretfully that the old way of the rope was better than the newer way of the law."[76]

Leibowitz faced a tough opponent in Alabama's attorney general, Thomas Knight Jr. A gifted lawyer, Knight's father, Thomas Knight Sr., had written the Alabama Supreme Court opinion upholding the first convictions.

When the defendants for the new trials were transferred first to a prison in Birmingham and then to Decatur's deplorable jail, the case's main figures had gathered for a renewed clash.

Chapter Five

Judge Horton's Courtroom

Before the next trial began, reporter F. Raymond Daniell from the *New York Times* visited Decatur to assess the mood but found little change from Scottsboro. A county official claimed that the men had already received one fair trial and added, "If this thing had happened twenty-five years ago there wouldn't have been any trial." He doubted any violence would occur unless "any N****** come around the courthouse and start acting up."[77] Daniell found it intimidating that every day the defense team and its witnesses would on its way to the courtroom pass by the stately monument of a Confederate soldier adorning the court's lawn.

Sheriff A.W. Davis hoped to forestall any outbursts. He planned to move in as many as seventy-five armed militiamen from surrounding communities to keep the peace, to search everyone going into the courtroom, and to allow inside only lawyers, the press, and people the sheriff personally knew.

Thomas G. Knight Jr. had launched an intense search for Ruby Bates. Though she had not been as strong a witness as Victoria Price, Knight needed her to buttress his case. However, the girl disappeared soon after the first trial and could not be located.

Judge James E. Horton Jr. would surprise many with his sense of justice and his adherence to duty. As he presided over the trial, he earned high marks for his qualities of decency, fairness, and compassion.

Into this swirl of emotions entered a judge who would introduce decency, fairness, and compassion to a case that had seen
little of these qualities so far. Judge James E. Horton Jr. had deep
ties to the South. Born in Alabama to a former slave owner and
to the daughter of a Confederate general, Horton entered the law
in 1899 and soon earned his community's respect with his flour-
ishing practice. Most observers thought that Horton would follow James F. Hawkins's example and preside over abrupt trials
ending with executions. They underestimated the man's devotion
to justice and his adherence to duty.

A sign came before the trial began when two black newspaper
reporters approached to thank him for arranging passes to the
court. In plain view Horton shocked residents by shaking their
hands and exchanging pleasantries. Such affable treatment was
not the norm for most white southerners.

The Trial Opens

Haywood Patterson's second trial started on March 30, 1933, when,
before a courtroom packed with 425 white onlookers, Samuel S.
Leibowitz moved to quash the charges on the basis that blacks had
been purposely excluded from the jury rolls. He interviewed twenty
prominent black residents, including two preachers, a dentist, and
a high school principal, to show that even though they were certainly qualified, they had never been called to serve on a jury.

Leibowitz's contention angered area citizens, who saw it as yet
another attack on their justice system. County jury commissioner
Arthur Tidwell testified that he had no idea whether blacks had
never served. "As long as I know he is a man of good character
and sound judgment, like it says in the law book, I put his name
in the box. I don't never ask whether he is a Negro or not and I
don't ever see them."[78] Because of the emotions this motion produced, Captain Joseph Burleson assigned five National Guard
troops to watch over the defense attorney.

Leibowitz correctly guessed that Horton would deny the motion, but he had entered it to set up grounds for a possible later
appeal to the Supreme Court. With the motion issue ended, a
jury was selected, and the case began in earnest.

Horton opened with a strong appeal that the jury set aside any
prejudices and do their duty. "So far as the law is concerned," he

said in a quiet, firm voice, "it knows neither native nor alien, Jew or Gentile, black or white. This case is no different from any other. We have only our duty to do without fear or favor." He added, "It would be a blot on the men and women of this country, a blot on all of you, if you were to let any act of yours mar the course of justice in this or any other case. Your fellow citizens would bow their heads in shame if any act of yours were to interrupt the course of justice." He ended his direction by reminding the twelve men, "We must be true to ourselves, and if we be true to ourselves we can't be false to any man."[79]

Price Testifies Again

On April 3 Price returned to the witness stand and repeated what she had said in Scottsboro. After Price's sixteen-minute testimony, Leibowitz cross-examined her for four hours, trying to discredit her by introducing evidence on her poor character, drawing attention to her contradictory statements, and showing the jury another version of what may have occurred on the train. Price replied in a sarcastic, taunting manner, causing Leibowitz to declare, "You're a little bit of an actress, aren't you?" Price retorted, "You're a pretty good actor yourself."[80]

Leibowitz's aggressive tactics backfired. Instead of convincing the court that Price could not be trusted, observers claimed that he solidified support for Price by treating her with disrespect. His questions "makes one feel like reaching for his gun while his blood boils to the nth degree," stated the Sylacauga *News*. One reporter overheard a spectator mutter, "It'll be a wonder if ever he leaves town alive."[81]

Word reached Horton from a National Guard undercover agent that more than two hundred angry people had met to decide on Leibowitz's fate. Various suggestions, including killing the lawyer and lynching the defendants, were discussed. The following day Horton had the jury removed so he could address the issue. Horton vowed that the court would protect the prisoners and that people who take the law into their hands "are citizens unworthy of the protection of the State of Alabama." Declaring, "I absolutely have no patience with mob spirit,"[82] Horton said the National Guard will do their duty and shoot to kill if needed to protect the prisoners.

I will say this much; so far as I am concerned I believe I am as gentle as any man in the world; I don't believe I would harm any one wrongfully, but when it comes to a question of right and wrong, when it comes to the very civilization, men no matter how quiet they are, or how peaceful they are, there comes a time when they must take a stand either right or wrong.[83]

Emotions cooled after Horton's forceful statement, even though his stance earned more enemies among people he had long known as neighbors. At least one man breathed easier. Patterson silently listened to the judge's warnings to Decatur's residents, words Patterson was convinced prevented a mass lynching.

Physicians in Court

R.R. Bridges, the Scottsboro physician who had examined Price and Bates, next testified. Though the prosecutor called him to the stand, Bridges provided ammunition for Leibowitz by claiming that the girls were unusually calm after the alleged attacks and showed few physical signs of being harmed.

After Bridges stepped down, his assisting physician, Marvin Lynch, was scheduled to follow. Before he took the stand Lynch approached Horton with the request to privately meet. While armed guards stood outside, Horton and Lynch disappeared into the courthouse restroom, where Lynch informed the judge he was convinced the girls were lying. Lynch added that when he said the same to the pair while examining them, they laughed.

"My God, Doctor, is this whole thing a horrible mistake?" asked Horton. "Judge," replied Lynch, "I looked at both the women and told them they were lying, that they knew they had not been raped, and they just laughed at me."[84] However, Lynch faced a dilemma. As a young physician establishing his practice, he stood to lose everything if he gave such an unpopular statement in court. Horton tried to convince him to testify, but Lynch feared the reaction he would receive from neighbors. "If I testified for those boys I'd never be able to go back into Jackson County."[85] Though he could have forced Lynch to appear, Horton was sympathetic and excused him from the case. The judge, who wondered about the validity of Price's testimony while being impressed with what Bridges said, placed his faith in the jury to sort out the evidence and arrive at a fair verdict.

The prosecutor called other witnesses to the stand. Arthur Woodall, a member of the posse that arrested the defendants at Paint Rock, said that he found a knife on one of the defendants who, upon being asked, said he took the knife from Price. Leibowitz's surprised look so delighted Knight that he clapped his hands and rushed out of court to hide his elation.

Dr. R.R. Bridges testified that when he examined the girls after the alleged attacks, they had been unusually calm and showed few signs of physical harm.

Ory Dobbins, who claimed he saw the fight as the train sped by his farm, followed. When Leibowitz asked how he could be so certain he saw two women on a train that passed by so quickly, Dobbins answered because they wore women's clothes. Leibowitz thought the answer helped his case as he and everyone else knew that the women wore coveralls instead of dresses.

Witnesses for the Defense

Leibowitz called a series of witnesses to punch holes in the state's case. Dallas Ramsey swore that he saw Price in a hobo jungle she said she had never visited. Lester Carter, a traveling companion

Brave Souls

———■———

Scottsboro featured the exploits of courageous individuals who battled for the rights of others and did what was right. Some of those, like the National Guard, were southerners who, even though they may not have liked their tasks, did what they were supposed to do. When Judge James E. Horton Jr. heard that a mob might break into the flimsy jail, lynch the nine Scottsboro Boys, and run Leibowitz out of town, Horton ordered the National Guard to shoot to kill at the first sign of trouble.

Captain John Burleson, commander of the National Guard detachment, never flinched, even though he faced the prospect of firing into a crowd containing friends and neighbors. "We'll be ready for them if they come," he told Horton. "Just because my men and I are Southerners and these prisoners are Negroes need not lead any one to think we won't do our duty. So long as we have a piece of ammunition or a man alive, those prisoners will be protected."

He explained to Horton that he would first have the fire department spray any crowd with cold water. He would turn to tear gas if water failed to disperse the mob, and employ bayonets and bullets only as a last resort. He told Horton that if it came to guns, his men would shoot to kill. Fortunately for the commander, he never had to institute such steps, but his willingness to do so exemplifies the bravery that some individuals display when confronted with injustice.

Quoted in F. Raymond Daniell. "Warning by Judge at Alabama Trial." *New York Times*, April 6, 1933.

of Price and Bates, testified that he and Jack Tiller had sex with Price and Bates in a hobo jungle near Huntsville two nights before the alleged rape. Other witnesses testified that the boarding-house Price claimed she and Bates stayed in did not exist, and that if a woman had been raped by at least six men, such a vicious assault would leave behind more signs than were seen on either Price or Bates when they were taken off the train.

Six of the Scottsboro Boys added their testimony. Willie Roberson claimed that he so badly suffered from venereal disease that he could not walk without a cane. When prosecutor Knight asked Patterson, "Were you tried in Scottsboro?" Patterson replied, "I was framed in Scottsboro." Knight asked who told him to say that, to which Patterson shot back, "I told myself to say it."[86]

Leibowitz's next witness stunned Horton, Knight, and most everyone else in the courtroom. After examining his final defense

In the second trial Ruby Bates (first row, second from right) denied being raped, saying she had gone along with Price because of fear of being arrested. Bates would later march in support of the defendants.

witness, Leibowitz asked for a brief recess. Minutes later National Guard troops with bayonets escorted Bates down the aisle. Horton stepped down from his bench to take a closer look as Bates walked to the front, spectators audibly gasped at the sight of the surprise witness, and Knight and his team looked as if they had seen a ghost.

As Price glared at her former companion, Bates explained that she had been so bothered by what she had done to the accused that she traveled to New York and consulted with the nationally renowned minister Harry Emerson Fosdick, whose name she had seen in a newspaper article. The religious leader advised her that if she wanted to ease her conscience, she had to return to Alabama and set the record straight. Bates promised to do so.

As a hushed courtroom listened to every word, Bates denied being raped and said that she had only gone along with the story when Price convinced her they would both be in trouble with the law unless they blamed the defendants. "I told it just like Victoria did because she said we might have to stay in jail if we did not frame up a story after crossing a state line with men."[87] In his cross-examination, Knight contended that she changed her story after being bribed to do so, evidence of which rested, he suggested, in the fashionable clothes she now mysteriously wore. When Knight asked Bates if he had not cautioned her at Scottsboro to tell the truth, Bates confirmed that he had.

Bates stepped down to a far different atmosphere than when she entered. Spectators resented her words and wondered how she could so blatantly lie rather than support her friend Price. They theorized that she had been bribed by the International Labor Defense (ILD) to alter her account. Emotion so intensified that the National Guard placed Bates under its protection and moved her to an unknown location for safety.

Summations

The intense emotions continued during the lawyers' summations. Prosecutor Wade Wright led off by insulting Leibowitz. "Show them that Alabama justice cannot be bought and sold with Jew money from New York!"[88] he shouted to the jury. Knight, embarrassed with his colleague's words, leaped to his feet to state he wanted no verdict based on prejudice, and Leibowitz moved for a mistrial. He

In his summation Leibowitz appealed to the jury, calling them logical and intelligent human beings, who were capable of giving a black man a square deal. His comments fell on deaf ears; the jury convicted Patterson in five minutes.

denied receiving money for the case and said, "When the hour of our country's need came," he said, referring to U.S. involvement in World War I from 1914 to 1918, "there was no question of Jew or Gentile, black or white. All, all together braved the smoke and flame of Flanders Field (scene of bitter fighting in France)."[89]

Horton denied the motion but cautioned jurors to ignore Wright's inflammatory words. Wright had appealed to emotions, and he had made an impact on the jury and gained favor with area citizens who feared that an acquittal would be a step toward granting social equality to blacks.

Leibowitz delivered a powerful summation, making a statement about his beliefs more than an emotional plea to the jury. "I shall appeal to your reason as logical, intelligent human beings, determined to give even this poor scrap of colored humanity a fair, square deal." He mentioned that during the course of the trial he had received many death threats, but said, "Mobs mean nothing to me. Let them hang me; I don't care. Life is only an incident in the Creator's scheme of things, but if I can contribute my little bit to see that justice is served, then my mission is fulfilled."[90]

On April 8 Horton issued his instructions to the jury. He said his "people have always been a Southern people, and I have no desire to live anywhere else. I am getting old, and it is my home, my native land, and I want to see righteousness done and justice done, and we are going to uphold that name." Horton asked them to examine the evidence and uncover the truth behind the statements so that they could arrive at a fair verdict. "We are a white race and a Negro race here together—we are here to live together—our interests are together. It seems sometimes that love has almost deserted the human bosom. It seems that hate has taken its place."[91]

The jury left to deliberate. From time to time laughter could be heard coming from the jury room, and when the jury returned the next day to deliver its verdict, Leibowitz was heartened that some on the jury smiled. The lawyer simply could not believe that a man could be laughing if he was sending someone to his death.

He erred. Foreman Eugene D. Bailey Jr. handed Horton a slip of paper with the guilty verdict. The members only required five minutes' debate to arrive at the conclusion but had taken the rest of the time arguing whether Patterson should be executed or placed in jail for the rest of his life. One juror held out for life imprisonment before being persuaded by the other eleven to vote for death. Horton thanked the jury for its work and ended the proceedings.

Angry Reactions

Though he had lost the trial, Leibowitz praised the judge and told Horton, "I am taking back to New York with me a picture of one of the finest jurists I have ever met."[92] He believed that had the verdict been left to Horton, his client would be free. As far as the jury was concerned, Leibowitz had little good to say. Becoming overly emotional, Leibowitz called the case "a black page in the history of American civilization."[93] He aired his frustrations with Alabama, saying,

> You must know this God-forsaken place, some of the creatures that live here, the mobs that burn crosses at night, masked like cowards so that decent people cannot see the sordidness and venom in their hideous countenances in order to understand that the verdict here was just a piece of judicial lynching.[94]

He added that his censure did not apply in any way to Horton, who "was like a straw caught in the whirlpool of bigotry and intolerance that surged through the court room, and his calm and judicious warnings to the twelve in the jury box could not have fallen upon understanding or willing ears."[95]

Leibowitz continued to attack Alabama upon his return to New York, where three thousand supporters greeted him at Pennsylvania Station. "If you ever saw those creatures, those bigots whose mouths are slits in their faces, whose eyes popped out at you like frogs, whose chins dripped tobacco juice, bewhiskered and filthy, you would not ask how they could do it."[96]

Though his irritation was understandable, Leibowitz handed ammunition to his southern opponents, who now claimed that while the lawyer criticized southerners as being prejudiced, he had proven with his words that he held bigoted beliefs of his own. Knight remarked that he and every southerner resented the inaccurate criticisms.

Horton's Courageous Act

On April 18 Patterson appeared before Horton to hear the sentence. When Horton asked if Patterson wished to speak, Patterson stated that he had been found guilty for a crime he did not commit. Horton issued the death sentence but suspended it due to a motion from the defense for a new trial. Horton then read a statement announcing that because of Leibowitz's inflammatory remarks, he was postponing the other trials until emotions calmed.

No Help from Washington

On May 7, 1933, Janie Patterson, Ruby Bates, and members of the ILD tried to arrange a meeting with President Franklin D. Roosevelt, hoping that a plea with the most powerful leader in the nation might result in a conclusion to the case. Louis Howe, one of Roosevelt's main advisers, said that as the president was then in a meeting with a German official, he could not see the group.

Patterson, Bates, and the others rejoined three thousand supporters outside the White House and marched down Pennsylvania Avenue to the Capitol, where Speaker of the House Henry T. Rainey and Vice President John Nance Garner met them. However, the group received little help from these politicians, who explained that they could not intervene in the case as it was a matter for the courts to decide.

The crowd dispersed, disappointed but not surprised that they had not found aid from the nation's political leaders in the controversial legal drama.

Janie Patterson and Ruby Bates joined three thousand Scottsboro Nine supporters in front of the White House on May 7, 1933.

Late the next month a man from the state's attorney general's office met with Horton. Rumors swirled that the judge might reverse the Patterson verdict, and the courier cautioned that such a step guaranteed Horton's loss in any reelection campaign. "What does that have to do with the case?" Horton asked. The messenger, who knew Horton's character, replied, "I told 'em you'd say that."[97]

On June 22 lawyers appeared before Horton to supposedly present arguments on a new trial, but instead for sixty-five minutes Horton read a 108-page typewritten statement pointing out ten errors in Price's testimony and referring to other evidence he believed cast doubt on Patterson's guilt. Despite knowing that his action would all but end his career, Horton set aside the verdict and ordered a new trial for Patterson.

Knight was visibly angered by Horton's words and promised to retry Patterson immediately, while Leibowitz praised what he called the "courageous" act. "I am glad for the sake of the poor parents of these boys, who have undoubtedly undergone as much, if not more, torture than the boys themselves."[98]

Many southern newspapers criticized Horton's act, while reaction elsewhere in the nation approved of what he had done. The nine defendants welcomed the surprise boost from a white southern judge, although Clarence Norris believed Horton should have dismissed the charges altogether and freed them. "I think Judge Horton was a brave man. He had the power. He could have ended our hell in 1933."[99]

Patterson, however, was overjoyed at receiving another chance. "His decision made me feel good. I saw there could be white folks in the South with a right mind."[100]

Horton stepped down from the case after being pressured by Chief Justice John C. Anderson. As predicted, Horton lost a 1934 reelection race, after which he retired to his law practice where he continued to be guided by the Horton family motto, "Let justice be done though the heavens may fall."[101]

A new judge was about to step in for yet another round of trials for nine black males who had been in jail since March 1931.

Chapter Six

A New Round of Trials

Prosecuting attorneys could not have been happier with Judge William W. Callahan. Whereas James E. Horton Jr. provided both sides equal opportunity to present their cases and worked toward a fair outcome, Callahan intended to end the trials as quickly as possible. He believed that Alabama had already wasted too much time and money on a case that, in his opinion, had turned embarrassing with its bickering lawyers and national spotlight on southern society. Friends of Callahan said the judge would handle the case the right way and make Alabamans proud. He made it clear he planned to have Haywood Patterson's trial over in three days.

The Judge

Callahan immediately set the tone by ruling that the defendants and their lawyers no longer required the protection of the National Guard. He claimed emotions had cooled, even though a series of lynchings and other violent actions in Alabama and elsewhere had recently occurred. One reporter wrote, "The scene and the very atmosphere of the court room is different and more tense than at any time in the previous trial,"[102] leading Samuel S. Leibowitz to appeal to both the state's governor and to President Franklin Roosevelt. Both leaders answered that protection in trials was a local matter and declined to step in.

Callahan imposed restrictions on reporters and photographers to reduce the number of spectators inside the courtroom and to curtail the amount of news coverage emanating from the room. Callahan felt that the press, with cameras flashing and typewriters clacking, had been an irritant in the earlier trials. He hoped to eliminate some of the distractions by banning photographers and typewriters from the courtroom and issuing clear instructions to reporters on how they were to conduct themselves.

In the third round of trials—as was the case in the earlier trials—the Scottsboro Boys had to be protected from violence by armed guards when they were taken from the jail to the courthouse.

On November 20, 1933 seven of the nine Scottsboro Boys entered the Decatur courtroom for a next round of testimony. Missing were Roy Wright and Eugene Williams who, as juveniles, had been transferred to juvenile court and remained in jail. Clarence Norris, already weary from a two-and-one-half year legal battle and imprisonment in brutal conditions, watched Callahan operate and concluded he stood no chance under the new judge. "This judge was a redneck from the word go," Norris contends. "His robes might as well have been those of the Ku Klux Klan. It didn't matter to him if we were innocent or guilty, he was determined to send us to the electric chair."[103]

The Trial Begins

The new round of trials began with Patterson, his third time in court for the alleged assault. Leibowitz opened by asking for a change of venue. He claimed that Morgan County's citizens had already been influenced by the earlier trials and that his clients could not receive a fair trial in Decatur. Prosecutor Thomas G. Knight Jr. replied by introducing sworn statements from local inhabitants saying that they had not been biased by what had happened earlier and that they could deliver a fair verdict. Callahan, whom reporters had nicknamed "Speedy" after his desire to keep the trial moving along, ruled the sworn statements were sufficient for him and denied Leibowitz's motion.

Leibowitz then amended his motion for a change of venue, arguing that a fair trial was impossible because no blacks in Morgan County had been placed on the jury rolls. How, he argued, could the defendants receive a fair trial if they were not judged by a jury of their peers? The state countered that the names of black citizens were on the rolls, but that not many qualified blacks existed. An Alabama jury commissioner testified,

> I do not know of any Negro in Morgan County over twenty-one and under sixty-five who is generally reputed to be honest and intelligent and who is esteemed in the community for his integrity, good character and sound judgment, who is not an habitual drunkard, who isn't afflicted with a permanent disease or physical weakness which would render him unfit to discharge the duties of juror and who can

read English and who has never been convicted of a crime involving moral turpitude.[104]

Leibowitz brought in a handwriting expert to prove that the few names of African American citizens had been fraudulently added after the jury pool had been selected. Once again, however, Callahan denied Leibowitz's motion.

Witnesses Take the Stand

Orville Gilley then took the witness stand. A hobo who described himself as a wandering poet, Gilley was riding in the same car as the young black men and Victoria Price and Ruby Bates. He supported Price's claim that she had been raped, but differed in a few areas. Whereas Price had sworn that Patterson had raped only her, Gilley said that Patterson had raped both girls and that, contrary to what Price claimed, no one held a knife to Price's neck. When Leibowitz wondered why Gilley had appeared in court only now, more than two years after the supposed incident, Knight admitted that he had sent money to both Gilley and his mother. Though Leibowitz believed this information helped his case, observers countered that the admission failed to make an impression on the jury.

Callahan gave Leibowitz little room in the lawyer's cross-examination of witnesses and introduction of new material, often objecting to what Leibowitz tried to do before Knight could rise out of his chair. As spectators shouted encouragement, Callahan admonished Leibowitz to move along to the next witness or question, or ruled that enough evidence had already been introduced on a particular issue.

Callahan severely restricted Leibowitz's case by refusing to allow him to introduce any information about Price's activities in the thirty-six hours before the alleged assault. Leibowitz wanted the jury to hear that the physical indications of sexual activity had come from her sex with Jack Tiller, not with Patterson, but Callahan ruled that as it occurred before the supposed rape, the incident was irrelevant to the case. Callahan's ruling also weakened R.R. Bridges's testimony about Price's physical condition.

"He kept helping the state prosecutor," said Patterson of Callahan. "He let the state people talk all they wanted. But he shut up

When hobo poet Orville Gilley took the stand, he testified that Patterson had raped both girls. This was Gilley's first appearance in a Scottsboro trial, but it would be revealed that prosecutor Knight had sent money to Gilley and his mother.

Leibowitz and the other Labor Defense lawyers every minute. Callahan would sometimes object himself before the state did."[105]

Though Leibowitz became more frustrated every time Callahan stepped in, the lawyer failed to grasp the insurmountable obstacles he faced in the South of the 1930s. As Norris writes, Leibowitz

> didn't understand that no matter what evidence he produced to the contrary, a Southern jury would never acquit a Negro of the charge of rape brought against him by a

white woman. It didn't matter whether the women had been raped or not, the code of the South at that time was that the word of the lowest white person was proof enough against the most influential black citizen.[106]

Patterson, nervous and constantly blinking his eyes, took the stand in his own behalf and swore that he had never seen any females on the train. He claimed that guards in jail threatened to hand him over to the mob outside unless he admitted the crime.

Leibowitz hoped to have Bates add her testimony, but Bates refused to return to Alabama after receiving a flood of hate mail threatening her with harm. The prosecution agreed with a proposal to have her give her statement in New York, but Bates fell ill and had to be rushed to the hospital. Callahan, already weary of the delay, refused to allow more time for Bates to recover and ordered lawyers to move on to other witnesses.

The Trial Ends

Leibowitz again upset the crowded courtroom in his summation by depicting Price as a person of low moral character and someone not to be trusted. As successful a lawyer as he was, Leibowitz never correctly assessed southern society. Residents may have quietly agreed that Price lacked character, but she was still a white woman under assault by black males. In their views, that could not easily be forgiven.

Callahan instructed the jury after lawyers concluded their summations. Often glaring at Leibowitz and others at the defense table, for two hours Callahan explained to the jurors their responsibilities under the law and what steps to take should they find Patterson guilty. "Where the woman charged to have been raped, as in this case, is a white woman," Callahan intoned, "there is a very strong presumption under the law that she will not and did not yield voluntarily to intercourse with the defendant, a Negro." Callahan added that this presumption that a white female would never willingly have intercourse with a black male was true no matter what her reputation, "whether she be the most despised, ignorant and abandoned woman of the community, or the spotless virgin and daughter of a prominent home of luxury and learning."[107] Callahan ended by telling the jurors they faced one of two choices if they found Patterson guilty—they could sentence him to be executed or give him imprisonment for anywhere from ten years to life.

After he finished, Leibowitz hurried to the bench and reminded the judge that he had overlooked a crucial matter—what the jury should do if it found Patterson innocent. Callahan tried to correct the glaring omission by admitting he had forgotten to deliver the instructions for acquittal, and told the jurors that if they had not been satisfied beyond a reasonable doubt that Patterson had committed the crime, they had a duty under the law to bring in a verdict of not guilty.

Not surprisingly, the jury found Patterson guilty and sentenced him to death. Patterson started to protest, then stopped. Some members of the jury hastily departed through a back door so they would not have to walk by Patterson.

Reaction in the South predictably agreed with the verdict. The *Memphis Commercial Appeal* said in December 1933 of the three Patterson trials, "About all that the Scottsboro case has demonstrated is that it is often a long time between a verdict of guilty and fulfillment of the court's sentence." The editors hoped the verdict would convince people around the nation that the sentences in all three trials had been correct and that the Alabama court system had properly conducted its duties. "But for the meddlesome interference of agencies outside the state the case of the seven Scottsboro defendants would have been disposed of in the usual manner long ago. The most extraordinary phase of the Scottsboro affair is the patience of Alabama courts and of Alabama citizens. None will ever be able to charge that there was hasty action."[108]

The second trial, that of Norris, followed shortly after Patterson's and concluded speedily with the same result. Before the third trial started, that of Charlie Weems, Leibowitz asked Callahan to postpone the remainder of the trials so he could appeal the Patterson and Norris verdicts to the Alabama Supreme Court and, eventually, the U.S. Supreme Court. Callahan agreed, starting the process that would send the cases back to the highest court in the land for the second time.

The nine faced yet more delays in their long ordeal. Patterson and Norris returned to death row at Kilby Prison, while the rest bided their time in the Birmingham jail and waited for the outcome

When a Person Goes Against the Crowd

People sometimes pay a heavy price for doing the right thing, especially when the actions go against public opinion. In Alabama a group of white leaders gathered at Birmingham and formed a coalition to support the nine Scottsboro Boys.

Two white males spoke at a May 26, 1933, rally on behalf of the accused. The speakers were Kenneth E. Barnhart, a professor of sociology at Birmingham-Southern College, and Rabbi Benjamin Goldstein of Temple Beth Or in Montgomery. Afterward, Barnhart's college failed to renew his contract for the next school year, even though his classes were among the most popular on campus. Goldstein received an ultimatum from his temple leaders to cut his connection to the Scottsboro case or resign the position he had long coveted. Both men received threats through the mail and by telephone.

Barnhart lost his teaching position, and Goldstein resigned. After moving to New York City, Goldstein said that anyone in the South who spoke out in any fashion favoring the Scottsboro Boys "is immediately branded a communist and a n*****-lover."

Quoted in Dan T. Carter. Scottsboro: *A Tragedy of the American South.* Baton Rouge: Louisiana State University Press, 1979, p. 259.

that one day in the not too near future would determine their fates. Some vented their frustrations by being surly and uncooperative. On March 25, 1934, the third anniversary of the alleged attack in the cargo train, the jail warden placed Williams, Andy and Roy Wright, Willie Roberson, and Ozie Powell in solitary confinement for infractions and disturbances, saying they had been a constant source of trouble since they arrived. The young men who had been separated from loved ones and from the outside world for such a long period could see no good end to this legal nightmare. "I wondered how much longer the state of Alabama would spend its money to prosecute nine innocent boys in order to send them to their deaths," writes Norris. "I couldn't understand it then or now, the hatred."[109]

Others continued to work on their behalf. Bates joined some of the defendants' mothers to visit the White House so they could

The all-white male jury received biased and racist instructions from Judge Callahan when they were charged with determining the verdict.

talk with Roosevelt about granting a pardon to free the men, but the president was supposedly in meetings and unavailable to see them. Patterson wrote two letters to the president but both times received a reply from one of Roosevelt's secretaries that the issue was a matter for Alabama to decide.

To Another Court

On May 25, 1934, Leibowitz presented his case to the Alabama Supreme Court, arguing that the convictions for Patterson and Norris should be set aside because blacks had been excluded from juries. Though the court's decision did not come for a month, Leibowitz was not surprised at the outcome. On June 28 the court declared that while no blacks had served on juries, they had not been excluded. The jury commission had simply chosen not to select them. The justices added that while Callahan might have been impatient in his desire to hasten the trials, he had not been unfair in his supervision of matters. The court denied Leibowitz's motion and set the execution date for the pair for August 31.

Leibowitz immediately appealed the decisions to the U.S. Supreme Court. Before the Supreme Court trial began, police in Huntsville, Alabama, arrested two International Labor Defense (ILD) attorneys on October 1, 1934, on charges of attempted bribery. The ILD had offered Price fifteen hundred dollars if she would sign a legal document stating that her earlier testimony was false. Price contacted the authorities, and the lawyers were arrested as they delivered the money.

Leibowitz exploded at the news and condemned the ILD's part in trying to illegally influence the witness. "I cannot continue as counsel in the Scottsboro case until the Communists are removed from all connection with the defense," said Leibowitz, who disavowed all knowledge of the event. "Until all secret maneuverings, ballyhoo, mass pressure and Communist methods are removed from the case, I can no longer continue. I am not deserting the Scottsboro boys. I have given of my best and am prepared to continue to do so to the end that the Scottsboro boys shall not die."[110]

A series of hastily arranged meetings produced a compromise. Leibowitz agreed to defend Norris, while the ILD handled Patterson's case.

The U.S. Supreme Court Decides

While the nine Scottsboro defendants remained in jail as the months dragged on, Leibowitz presented his case to the U.S. Supreme Court on February 15, 1935. He argued that the verdicts must be set aside because blacks had been purposely excluded from serving on Alabama juries. When the justices asked if he had any proof, Leibowitz replied that that an inspection of the jury rolls would show evidence of tampering. For the first time in the court's history, the justices asked that evidence be brought into their courtroom. One by one the justices examined the rolls, each reacting in shock at the names of black residents that had been illegally scribbled in to make it appear they had been present before bringing Patterson and Norris to trial. Knight attempted to counter the damaging evidence by arguing that blacks had simply not been selected to serve on juries, but the justices appeared to disregard his words.

Chief Justice Charles Evans Hughes delivered the court's decision on April 1, 1935. In *Norris* v. *Alabama* the court declared that every citizen in the United States enjoyed equal protection under the law as provided by the Fourteenth Amendment to the U.S. Constitution and that preventing blacks from serving on juries violated that right. The court was convinced that the names of black residents had been illegally added to the jury rolls after the juries had been selected, and it pointed to the Alabama jury commissioner who said that he knew no black in Morgan County worthy of being chosen as proof of a prevailing atmosphere that denied blacks their basic rights. As a result of these violations of

In *Norris v. Alabama*, Supreme Court justice Charles Evans Hughes wrote the Court's decision, stating that every citizen in the United States enjoyed equal protection under the law as provided in the Fourteenth Amendment to the Constitution. He went on to say that preventing blacks from serving on juries violated that right, and he ordered new trials.

Leibowitz's Legacy

Samuel Leibowitz's enduring legacy includes the fact that before the *Norris v. Alabama* decision, African Americans were being prevented from serving on southern juries. The decision made clear that, by federal law, they could serve.

A few years after the Scottsboro cases ended, Samuel S. Leibowitz vacationed in Florida. Wherever he traveled, the attorney loved to visit courtrooms to observe other lawyers and judges in action, thinking that he might learn something of value for his own work. When he spotted a black member on a Miami jury, Leibowitz asked the defense counsel about the man's presence, as he did not think black jurors were very common in the South.

"Yes, it is something new," the Florida attorney replied. "This is the first time in our state we have had a n***** on a jury and it's all on account of a son-of-a-bitch named Leibowitz from New York. He came down to Alabama a few years ago to try a case and somehow he got to the Supreme Court in Washington, and damned if we haven't had to put n***** on our juries ever since."

Rather than being upset by the Florida lawyer's comments, Leibowitz was proud that he had helped make gains for black citizens in the South.

Quoted in Quentin Reynolds. *Courtroom: The Story of Samuel S. Leibowitz*. New York: Farrar, Straus, 1950, p. 248.

Patterson's and Norris's rights under the Fourteenth Amendment, the justices ordered new trials and called on Alabama officials to correct the injustice.

Reaction to the Supreme Court's decision predictably varied according to the source. The *New York Times* printed that even newspapers in Great Britain hailed the outcome and praised the decision as proof that the court "is anxious to secure and protect the rights of the humblest citizen."[111] Representing calmer opinions in the South, the *Birmingham Age-Herald* wrote that it "sees no reason for great alarm as a result"[112] of the decision. Safeguards existed to prevent unqualified persons serving on juries whether they were white or black. The *Montgomery Advertiser* typified a harsher southern view. "The *Advertiser* may be dumb, as well as 'lost and ruint,' but to save itself it cannot see what the political rights and privileges of Negroes in Alabama have to do with the guilt or innocence of the gorillas who are charged with criminal assault upon two women, it being agreed that rape is a felony under the law in this backward State."[113]

In Alabama, Governor Bibb Graves ordered all state courts to obey the decision. He explained, "Holdings of the United States Supreme Court are the supreme law of the land. Whether we like the decision or not, it is the patriotic duty of every citizen and the sworn duty of every public officer to accept and uphold them in letter and spirit."[114] Graves mailed a notice to every court explaining that he was not implying that any particular judge or jury commissioner had been purposely excluding blacks, he was only asking that they take steps to ensure it did not happen in the future. Alabama, he added for emphasis, would obey the ruling.

Change was happening in Alabama but not swiftly enough for the nine defendants. While Leibowitz and Knight argued before various judges, and while state officials implemented alterations in jury selection, the nine remained incarcerated. Each day of the process meant another day behind bars for Patterson, Norris, and their companions.

Chapter Seven

The Long Ordeal Ends

For four long years the state of Alabama had attempted to prove the Scottsboro Boys' guilt to the world. Though different juries had delivered similar verdicts, outside the South few people believed they had committed any crime. A series of steps ended the legal dilemma, only to send the Scottsboro Nine into another strange world.

Haywood Patterson Again Guilty

For the next round of trials, the International Labor Defense (ILD) decided that it needed a lawyer that people in the South would be more willing to accept. In December 1935 it again joined with the National Association for the Advancement of Colored People (NAACP), as well as a few other organizations working to free the men, to create the Scottsboro Defense Committee. Condemned from the start as an outsider, Samuel S. Leibowitz's aggressive handling of the case, which included his unrelenting questioning of Victoria Price's character, had offended southerners, and at the ILD's suggestion he agreed to step to the background and allow a local attorney, Charles Watts, to be the chief defense lawyer. Leibowitz assented in the hope that his clients might receive a more favorable ruling from the next jury.

In the next trial Haywood Patterson was again found guilty, although he was not sentenced to death. Leibowitz told him this was a victory, but Patterson could not agree. He faced seventy-five years in prison for a crime he had not committed.

Because of the recent Supreme Court decision, the jury pool for Haywood Patterson's fourth trial included twelve blacks out of the one hundred men called for duty. Nervous over what local whites might do to them or their families if they served, seven of the twelve blacks asked to be excused for personal reasons. When during his questioning the prosecutor rejected the other five as unacceptable, each breathed a sigh of relief and hurried out of court. Rather than being upset that fellow blacks wanted nothing to do with the trial, Patterson understood. "That was okay with me," he said. "I didn't want no scared Negroes judging me."[115]

On January 21, 1936, police escorted Patterson into William W. Callahan's court for yet another trial to determine his guilt or innocence. Before national reporters, by now tired of witnessing the same drama, and Alabama citizens, who had grown weary of the whole matter, Price and other people repeated their stories, and Callahan restricted what the defense team could do. One new witness, Obie Golden, a guard at Kilby Prison, claimed that Patterson had once confessed to him that he had committed a crime, but under cross-examination he could give no reason why Patterson might have willingly admitted such a thing to a guard and could not say what crime Patterson supposedly confessed to.

The Fourteenth Amendment

The U.S. Supreme Court turned to the Fourteenth Amendment to the U.S. Constitution as a reason for ruling that the Scottsboro Boys had been denied their basic rights. Ratified on July 9, 1868, the amendment was one of a handful of new amendments that helped establish basic rights for recently liberated slaves after the Civil War (1861–1865). It granted complete citizenship to any person, male or female, born in the United States, including those former slaves, and forbade any state from denying "life, liberty or property, without due process of law" or to deny to any person residing in the state the "equal protection of the laws." The amendment purposely directed its message to individual states, especially those from the former Confederacy in the South that had rebelled during the Civil War, and thus enlarged the role of the federal government in ensuring individual rights.

Correctly assessing the state's mood, Morgan County prosecutor Melvin C. Hutson told the jury in his summation that every woman in Alabama looked to them to protect them, and that if they freed Patterson not only would they have to face their neighbors but every female would "have to go around with six-shooters" for protection. "Don't go out and quibble over the evidence. Say to yourselves 'we're tired of this job' and put it behind you. Get it done quick and protect the fair womanhood of this great State."[116]

Watts countered the emotional appeal with a calm summation of the facts and an appeal to reason. "It takes courage to do the right thing in the face of public clamor for the wrong thing, but when justice is not administered fairly, governments disintegrate and there is no protection for any one, man or woman, black or white."[117]

As the jury filtered from the courtroom, every onlooker expected the same result—a guilty verdict with a death sentence attached. Observers proved half right. This jury differed from the previous ones in that one member was not convinced Patterson deserved to die. John Burleson, a devout Methodist, believed Patterson might have committed the crime but that he had not started the brawl and had been tempted by Price and Ruby Bates. For hours he debated with his eleven companions, who favored execution and feared what might happen when they returned to their hometowns if they declared Patterson innocent. Finally, exhausted from the ordeal, Burleson compromised. Despite his doubts he would agree to a guilty verdict if the eleven assented to a sentence of seventy-five years in prison. Burleson later explained that he agreed to vote guilty because he thought the case against Patterson was so weak that as soon as emotions calmed, Patterson would be released from prison.

When the jury foreman announced the sentence, Thomas G. Knight Jr., who like most everyone else expected another sentence of death, looked as if he had been punched in the stomach. Leibowitz reacted with glee, told Patterson he had just won a victory and would continue to labor for his freedom. When Patterson wondered how seventy-five years in prison for a crime he had not committed was a victory, Leibowitz tried to explain that this was the first time an Alabama jury had declined to send a black rapist to the electric chair.

Patterson took little solace in his lawyer's words. All he could see was a life behind bars for something he did not do. "It was no victory for me," he said. "I knew I was going to be driven to a slow death. I knew that Alabama would never let me go free." Rather than enduring seven decades of torment, he preferred to be executed and be done with the entire matter. "These people didn't know what the Alabama prisons were like. I already had a five-year taste of it. It was living death."[118]

Deputies returned a confused and angry Patterson to his cell while his lawyers congratulated each other for opening what they considered the first wedge in the southern court system. They considered it a partial victory only and planned to appeal this decision as they had with the other verdicts.

An Incident Mars the Decision

While the defense team congratulated itself on reaching the different verdict, violence erupted. On January 24, 1936, Ozie Powell and two others were being driven from the trial in Decatur back to the Birmingham jail by Deputy Sheriff Edgar Blalock and Sheriff J. Street Sandlin. Clarence Norris sat in the middle of the backseat, handcuffed to Powell on his right with Powell's right hand free and Roy Wright to Norris's left with Wright's left hand free. Powell had a knife hidden in the crotch of his pants.

Sheriff Sandlin drove the vehicle while Blalock sat on the passenger side. Blalock started taunting the three, saying they would have been better off with southern lawyers and that every one of them should have been killed years earlier. Infuriated at the words, Powell retrieved his weapon with his free hand and reached around and slashed Blalock's throat.

As blood gushed, Sandlin pulled the car to the side of the road, stepped out, and shot wildly through the open window at the three men. The sheriff was prepared to fire again when a car with prosecuting attorney Knight pulled up. Sandlin explained that Powell tried to escape and that he had shot him in an attempt to prevent it. Norris and Wright disputed the sheriff's contention that Powell had tried to escape. They claimed that they would never take such a step right after Patterson had avoided the death penalty.

Powell and Blalock both survived the incident. A physician used ten stitches to patch Blalock's wound and released him that day. Powell barely avoided dying from the bullet that went through his head but miraculously did not kill him. Powell, however, was never the same. "His personality was totally different," said Norris. "It seemed as if he was in a daze or something. He paid a high cost for our dignity as black men."[119]

By now many white Alabamans had wearied of the case, the cost of the trials and protection, and the critical views many in the nation and around the world held of them. A reporter talked with Alabama citizens and found that while they were divided on the issue of guilt, they were united in a strong desire for the case to be resolved.

Episcopalian bishop William G. McDowell wrote to the American Civil Liberties Union (ACLU) that the verdict showed "a remarkable change of sentiment" in Alabama and that it was the first time anyone there could recall where "a negro convicted of criminal assault on a white woman was not sentenced to death."[120]

The nine defendants saw things differently. Now in jail for almost five years, they began despairing of ever receiving a fair verdict. Powell's mother, Josephine, drove from Atlanta to see him after the car attack and found her son in a deep depression. When she walked in, Powell sat up and cried. "I done give up," he said. "I feel like everybody in Alabama is down on me and is mad with me."[121]

A Compromise Appears

Before the trials of the remaining young men took place, events occurred behind the scenes throughout 1936 that would have a dramatic impact on the Scottsboro Nine's futures. Negotiations to work out a compromise between the prosecution and the defense began during the summer of 1936. In December of that year Knight traveled to New York City for a secret meeting with Leibowitz.

Always attuned to the political mood of his state, Knight sensed that his voters wanted the long ordeal over. Earlier emotions had cooled, and most preferred to get back to their lives and forget about the Scottsboro Nine. "This damn case is costing the taxpayers of Alabama a lot of money," Knight said to Leibowitz. "It is proving itself a nuisance politically and every other way. We're sick and tired of the Scottsboro boys, let's sit down and find some solution to the case that will satisfy you and allow us to save face."[122]

As part of the compromise reached by the prosecution and defense, Roberson, Montgomery, Roy Wright, and Williams (pictured with attorney Sam Leibowitz) toast being released, but the other five defendants remained in prison.

Leibowitz attempted to get all charges dropped against Olen Montgomery, Willie Roberson, Eugene Williams, and Roy Wright. Leibowitz offered that the four on trial would plead guilty to simple assault and be released shortly afterward. Knight proposed to free them if Patterson and Norris pleaded guilty to rape. The meeting ended without a decision, but over the next few weeks Knight and Leibowitz bargained back and forth. Negotiations between state attorneys and the defense continued, prodded by public sentiment for a solution, even after Knight died in May 1937. On June 12, 1937, the editor of the *Montgomery Advertiser* called for a compromise so that Alabama could finally be freed from the harsh criticism that had assailed it since 1931, stating that the state's good name was worth more than whatever happened to the nine defendants. "Throw this body of death away from Alabama,"[123] boldly urged the editor.

The Alabama Supreme Court again upheld Patterson's conviction on June 14. Trials for the other men began in July. Norris, Andy Wright, Charlie Weems, and Powell all were found guilty, but only Norris received the death sentence. The others were given prison terms of anywhere from twenty years to ninety-five years. At this time the two sides finally agreed to a compromise. The five men already convicted—Patterson, Norris, Wright, Weems, and Powell—would remain in jail, as the state considered them the ringleaders of the alleged assault, but all charges against the other four would be dropped. The prosecution contended that Willie Roberson and Olen Montgomery were physically unable to commit the crime and that additional punishment was unnecessary for Roy Wright and Eugene Williams, juveniles who had already spent more than six years in prison. Based on the same evidence, four men walked out of jail free men while five others remained incarcerated.

When news of the compromise broke, Leibowitz declared victory and celebrated the end of Alabama's efforts to execute those four clients. Leibowitz said, "It is nothing short of a miracle that the boys were saved from the chair, and it's God's wonder that they are actually free. I can hardly believe it. We'll keep up the fight until all of these innocent boys are saved."[124] Before the local residents had time to react, Callahan ordered the state police to escort Leibowitz and the four freed men to the state line, where they were no longer under Alabama jurisdiction.

The five who remained in prison believed Leibowitz and the defense team had sold them out and won freedom for the other four at the cost of their confinement. Norris argued that if a deal had not been arranged, his four companions would still be in jail "serving time for something they didn't do." He added somberly that while the other defendants enjoyed their freedom, "I am in the same shape that I was in in 1931."[125]

Norris wrote bitterly to one of the lawyers. "I say you all framed me to the Electric Chair and the others in prison with a lifetime for the freedom of the other four boys." He added, "I have got tired of seeing peoples using me for the good of others. I just soon be dead than to be treated like I have been treated by you all. I believe all of you all just as much against me as that old lying woman that caused me to suffer near seven years."[126]

Patterson summed it up in simple terms. "They called this settlement a victory. For the boys let off it was a victory. For those of us dealt off it was something else."[127]

Similar Worlds

The four freed men accompanied Leibowitz to New York City, where a large crowd of supporters welcomed them. After the warm greeting, they quickly discovered that they had been drastically changed by their experiences in the past six years. Although no longer in jail, they would continue to pay a heavy price for what happened in Scottsboro. For the remainder of their lives they had problems adjusting to life as free men.

They first took issue with how Leibowitz treated them. The lawyer, eager to shield the men from people trying to take advantage, controlled what they did and to whom they talked. One month later, eager to earn some money so they could help their parents and enjoy a bit of life, they broke away and agreed to let Thomas Harten, a black minister with a shady past, manage their affairs. Harten arranged an appearance at the famous Apollo Theater in New York, for which the four were promised an ample payment, but after Harten and the theater deducted their shares, the four had little to show for the effort.

Their difficulties failed to match the misery endured by the five men still behind bars. While the others remained at Kilby, Alabama authorities sent Patterson to Atmore Prison, a nightmarish place filled with violence and poison snakes designated as the place to which wardens of other prisons sent their worst prisoners.

In December 1937 Patterson appealed to the highest authority in the land when he wrote a letter to President Franklin Roosevelt.

> I suppose you are president of this country and if so you are president of the state of Alabama as well. I am a citizen of America that has always been square toward every man and paid my bills as they accrued. I now ask you in return to intervene and protect me in my rights. I have never been guilty of any bad crime or open defiance of the law and yet I am unable to get a square deal.[128]

A second letter Patterson sent to his lawyers the next month dripped with guilt, not over committing a crime, but for what the seven years had done to his parents, who recently passed away. "I am a double murder," he wrote. "I was the cause of my father's death about 10 months ago and my darling mother now." What hounded him was that he now could no longer "ask them to forgive for all the miserable heartaches and sorrows and heavy burdens I caused them to bear."[129]

In March 1938 an inmate with a knife attacked Andy Wright and Weems. "Help Help," a friend of Wright's wrote his lawyer, "its lashing its slashing its slow cold blood murder down here at Kilby for we."[130] No help came. When he continued to pester the ILD for assistance, Wright received the same refrain—he needed to be patient because things took time—prodding him to reply in 1943 that he wearied of hearing "the same old theme about it takes time and I have been listening at that song for 12 long years."[131]

The freed men arrive in New York City's Penn station to be greeted by a crowd of three thousand supporters.

A Broadway Play

Poets, essayists, and newspaper reporters made Scottsboro the subject of hundreds of articles and poems. Hollywood and television studios produced films about the subject, and in New York City a 2011 Broadway production made Scottsboro the central theme.

As early as 1934 a play had come to Broadway. Written by John Wexley, *They Shall Not Die* attempted to bring the drama of the Alabama case to New York audiences. Wexley had already gained fame for writing a play about prison, *The Last Mile*, which introduced a young Spencer Tracy to national praise, and he hoped to educate Americans to the racial situation in the South. As preparation, Wexley had read the court records and interviewed lawyers involved with the case as well as Ruby Bates.

The play opened at the Royale Palace in New York on February 21, 1934, featuring renowned actors such as Claude Rains, Tom Ewell, and Ruth Gordon. Besides his views on the racial issue, Wexley, using Samuel S. Leibowitz as his vehicle, tackled the prevailing anti-Semitic attitudes some in the nation then held.

Wexley's message hit home with audiences. Broadway newspaper critic Robert Garland of the *New York World Telegram* wrote, "Not in all my theatergoing days have I seen such righteous indignation in the theater. A righteous indignation that, like a spark along a fuse, runs from play to player, from player to audience." Some attendees even wrote letters to Alabama's governor asking fair play for the nine defendants.

Quoted in James A. Miller. *Remembering Scottsboro*. Princeton, NJ: Princeton University Press, 2009, p. 100.

For a time in 1938 it appeared the men might receive a pardon. On October 29 Alabama governor Bibb Graves conducted interviews with the five, but concluded that they were too unrepentant to be released. Patterson hurt his chances by bringing a concealed knife into the meeting. Powell refused to answer any of Graves's questions, and Norris appeared rebellious and insolent.

Freedom for All

The five eventually left jail. Alabama pardoned Weems in November 1943, twelve years after being apprehended. He told reporters outside Kilby that he hoped to put everything aside, work hard, and be a productive man. Powell was paroled in June 1946, two years before Patterson escaped from Atmore and made his way north.

Andy Wright and Norris, whose death sentences had been reduced to life in prison in July 1938, received their paroles in January 1944 and were ordered to remain in Alabama. When they did not, authorities promised not to prosecute them if they returned but reneged on the deal when the pair did show up in Alabama. Norris was paroled again in 1946. He broke parole again by leaving the state, but this time he was not caught. Four years later Andy Wright was freed. Though he suffered abuse those long years, Wright felt no bitterness, telling reporters, "I have no hard feelings toward anyone. I'm not mad because the girl lied about me. If she's still living, I feel sorry for her because I don't guess she sleeps much at night."[132]

The five experienced the same problems as their four cohorts earlier released—freedom from jail did not necessarily mean freedom from problems. One of the defense attorneys, Allan Chalmers, wrote that the trials and incarcerations had taken a heavy toll on the nine, and that even though they were out of jail "they are probably already too ruined by this experience to adjust to life in this already maladjusted world."[133]

Montgomery beseeched Chalmers and others for help to reenter a society he little knew or understood. After leaning on Leibowitz and the ILD for years, he now had to make it on his own in a hard world. He wanted to be an independent man, but troubled from the onset, he turned to alcohol as a solution.

"I am just like a rabbit in a strange wood and the dogs is after him and no place to hide," Andy Wright wrote Chalmers in 1950. Without friends or family in Albany where he lived, "Freedom don't mean a thing to me."[134] The next year a woman falsely accused Wright of raping her thirteen-year-old daughter. Even though he was found innocent, Wright spent another eight months in prison for a crime he had not committed. Andy's brother, Roy, joined the army and married. In 1959, after returning home to find his wife, Kathleen, had been unfaithful, Roy shot and killed her, then committed suicide.

Only Norris took official steps to restore his good name. Norris married Melba Sanders, with whom he had two daughters, and worked as a vacuum sweeper for New York City. He decided to seek a formal pardon when his girls read an article about the case and asked if he was the man in the article. In 1976 he applied for a full pardon from then Alabama governor George Wallace. "I was tired of being a fugitive," he explained. "I want to clear the record. I don't want my family bothered or worried. I want to be able to take them any place in this country."[135] Hoping to nudge the case further into the past, Wallace agreed and signed a pardon. Norris died in 1989 at the age of seventy-six.

Williams and Roberson eventually settled down to new lives. Williams moved to St. Louis, Missouri, to live with relatives, and Roberson worked for a time as a mechanic in New York. Their dates of death are unknown, but plagued with an asthma condition made worse by his six years in jail, Roberson died from an asthma attack. Montgomery struggled to find decent work and moved to Detroit, Michigan, to live with his sister. While there a female accused him of rape, but police dropped the charges before the case went to trial. He returned to Monroe, Georgia, the town of his birth, and died at an unknown date.

Patterson's turbulent life continued outside prison walls. He fled to Michigan to live with family but was apprehended by the FBI in 1950. Convinced that Patterson had suffered enough, Michigan governor G. Mennen Williams declined to sign legal papers that would force Patterson to return to Alabama. In December of that year, however, Patterson was arrested for murder after a fight in a bar resulted in a stabbing death. He was convicted of manslaughter and sentenced to a term of six to fifteen years in jail, but Patterson never served his complete time. On August 24, 1961, Patterson died from cancer, ending his life in a yet another jail cell.

Life offered little comfort to Price or Bates. Price disappeared for years, resurfacing as Katherine Queen Victory Street to sue a television network over a movie about the case that it produced and broadcast. A judge dismissed her suit, and Price died in 1982. After working in an upstate New York spinning factory, Bates developed tuberculosis and returned to Huntsville to live with her mother. Bates moved to the state of Washington in 1940, married Elmer Schut, and resettled as Lucille Schut. Bates died in October 1976.

While the nine defendants struggled in their posttrial lives, those who best thrived after the trials were the lawyers and prosecutors involved in the incident, a lesson not lost on Norris. "And most of the officials involved with the case tried to use it as a stepladder to success; reputations were won or lost," he writes. "Organizations became larger and better known. Newspapers sold better, deputies became sheriffs, elected officials were re-elected and went on to bigger and better positions."[136]

Knight gained one of Alabama's top posts, and Leibowitz returned to New York to great acclaim, continued to build his successful legal career, and became a New York Supreme Court justice before dying in January 1978. Only James E. Horton Jr., who so admirably stood up for truth and justice when some called for vengeance and blood, suffered for his actions. After losing his earlier election on account of his role in the trial, Horton retired to private practice and his family's plantation, where he died in 1973 at the age of ninety-five.

Posttrial Publicity

A handful of books, films, and documentaries have appeared in the intervening decades, some written by the individuals involved. In 1950 Patterson published his autobiography, *Scottsboro Boy*, a searing account of his life in Alabama prisons. Norris published *The Last of the Scottsboro Boys* in 1979, a less-emotional assessment of the case and life afterward.

The National Broadcasting Company (NBC) aired the made-for-television film *Judge Horton and the Scottsboro Boys* in 1976, leading to unsuccessful lawsuits by both Price and Bates, who were angered with how the film portrayed them. The film gained praise for its sympathetic view of the case and for giving public notice to Horton's bravery. The famous blues singer Lead Belly recorded the song "Scottsboro Boys," and in 2011 the play *The Scottsboro Boys* appeared on Broadway in New York City, proof that interest in the 1931 incident has not faded.

The most acclaimed project to trace its origins, at least in part, to Scottsboro is the 1960 book and subsequent film *To Kill a Mockingbird*, written by Harper Lee. Constructed around the supposed rape by a black male of a white woman in the South, the book sold millions of copies and was named in a 1991 survey as

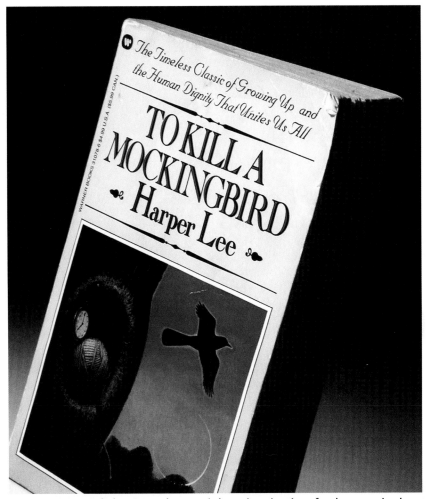

Harper Lee used the Scottsboro trials as inspiration for her seminal American literary work *To Kill a Mockingbird.*

one of the three most influential books, second only to the Bible. Lee, who was born in the small town of Monroeville in southwest Alabama, used the Scottsboro Boys as inspiration for a book that has become required reading in many high schools.

That Scottsboro created such a legacy is not surprising, for it is a tale for the ages, offering heroism as well as tragedy, nobility, and corruption. The two U.S. Supreme Court rulings that came from the trials solidified individual rights as they pertained to

The cast from the 2011 musical *The Scottsboro Boys* performs at the 2011 Tony Awards.

court cases. Combined with widespread news coverage of the events, they helped build momentum for the civil rights movement that rocked the nation in the 1950s and contributed to the decline of an antiquated system based upon the notion of white supremacy.

When a reporter asked Leibowitz what the case meant to him, he had a ready reply. "What did the Scottsboro case mean to me? Well, I like to think that I helped a little in convincing the public that a Negro is a citizen, entitled to the full privileges of citizenship." He said that as a result, he believed the South was changing. "Yes, I had a little to do with that, and that's what the Scottsboro case means to me."[137]

In 1976 Norris had a more direct message, not only to his race but to every man, woman, and child. "The lesson to black people, to my children, to everybody is that you should always fight for your rights, even if it costs you your life. Stand up for your rights, even if it kills you."[138]

Notes

Chapter One: A Tragic Train Ride

1. Clarence Norris and Sybil D. Washington. *The Last of the Scottsboro Boys*. New York: G.P. Putnam's Sons, 1979, p. 9.
2. Quoted in Kwando Mbiassi Kinshasa. *The Man from Scottsboro*. Jefferson, NC: McFarland, 1997, p. 36.
3. Quoted in Kinshasa, *The Man from Scottsboro*, p. 37
4. Haywood Patterson and Earl Conrad. *Scottsboro Boy*. Garden City, NY: Doubleday, 1950, p. 9.
5. Quoted in James Goodman. *Stories of Scottsboro*. New York: Pantheon, 1994, p. 17.
6. Hollace Ransdell. "Report on the Scottsboro, Ala. Case." American Civil Liberties Union, May 27, 1931, p. 18. www.law.umkc.edu/faculty/projects/FTrials/scottsboro/Scottsbororeport.pdf.
7. Quoted in Goodman. *Stories of Scottsboro*, p. 5.
8. Quoted in Goodman. *Stories of Scottsboro*, p. 19.
9. Norris and Washington. *The Last of the Scottsboro Boys*, pp. 21–22.
10. Quoted in Dan T. Carter. *Scottsboro: A Tragedy of the American South*. Baton Rouge: Louisiana State University Press, 1979, p. 13.
11. Quoted in Carter. *Scottsboro: A Tragedy of the American South*, p. 13.
12. Norris and Washington. *The Last of the Scottsboro Boys*, p. 22.
13. Quoted in Carter. *Scottsboro: A Tragedy of the American South*, p. 18.
14. Ransdell. "Report on the Scottsboro, Ala. Case," pp. 18–19.
15. Ransdell. "Report on the Scottsboro, Ala. Case," pp. 18–19.
16. Quoted in Ransdell. "Report on the Scottsboro, Ala. Case," p. 19.
17. Quoted in Arthur Garfield Hays. *Trial by Prejudice*. New York: Civici Friede, 1933, p. 37.

Chapter Two: The First Round of Trials

18. Quoted in Norris and Washington. *The Last of the Scottsboro Boys*, p. 23.
19. Ransdell. "Report on the Scottsboro, Ala. Case," pp. 3, 5.
20. Ransdell. "Report on the Scottsboro, Ala. Case," p. 14.
21. Ransdell. "Report on the Scottsboro, Ala. Case," p. 14.
22. Ransdell. "Report on the Scottsboro, Ala. Case," pp. 15–16.
23. Quoted in Kinshasa. *The Man from Scottsboro*, p. 41.

24. Quoted in Douglas O. Linder. "The Trials of 'The Scottsboro Boys.'" Famous AmericanTrials, pp. 2–3. http://law2.umkc.edu/faculty/projects/FTrials/scottsboro/SB_acct.html.

25. Quoted in F. Raymond Daniell. "Negro Lad Tells Scottsboro Story." *New York Times*, March 10, 1933.

26. Quoted in Linder. "The Trials of 'The Scottsboro Boys,'" p. 3.

27. Patterson and Conrad. *Scottsboro Boy*, p. 13.

28. Quoted in Goodman. *Stories of Scottsboro*, p. 16.

29. Ransdell. "Report on the Scottsboro, Ala. Case," p. 8.

30. Quoted in Patterson and Conrad. *Scottsboro Boy*, p. 249.

31. *New York Times*. "Deny Negroes' Trial Is Legal Lynching." April 9, 1931.

32. *New York Times*. "Deny Negroes' Trial Is Legal Lynching."

33. *New York Times*. "Deny Negroes' Trial Is Legal Lynching"

34. Quoted in Norris and Washington. *The Last of the Scottsboro Boys*, p. 24.

35. Quoted in James R. Acker. *Scottsboro and Its Legacy*. Westport, CT: Praeger, 2008, p. 34.

Chapter Three: Legal Battles

36. Quoted in Goodman. *Stories of Scottsboro*, p. 6.

37. Quoted in Acker. *Scottsboro and Its Legacy*, p. 36.

38. Quoted in Carter. *Scottsboro: A Tragedy of the American South*, p. 106.

39. Quoted in Goodman. *Stories of Scottsboro*, p. 83.

40. Quoted in Carter. *Scottsboro: A Tragedy of the American South*, p. 58.

41. Quoted in Goodman. *Stories of Scottsboro*, p. 84.

42. Quoted in Goodman. *Stories of Scottsboro*, p. 84.

43. Quoted in Norris and Washington. *The Last of the Scottsboro Boys*, pp. 58–59.

44. Quoted in Carter. *Scottsboro: A Tragedy of the American South*, p. 107.

45. Files Crenshaw Jr. and Kenneth A. Miller. *Scottsboro: The Firebrand of Communism*. Montgomery, AL: Brown, 1936, p. 9.

46. Quoted in John Temple Graves II. "Alabama Resents Outside Agitation." *New York Times*, June 21, 1931, p. 31.

47. Quoted in Carter. *Scottsboro: A Tragedy of the American South*, p. 136.

48. Quoted in Carter. *Scottsboro: A Tragedy of the American South*, p. 136.

49. Quoted in Irving Stone. *Clarence Darrow for the Defense*. Garden City, NY: Garden City, 1943, p. 497.

50. Quoted in Goodman. *Stories of Scottsboro*, p. 8.

51. Quoted in Kinshasa. *The Man from Scottsboro*, pp. 43, 50.

52. Quoted in *New York Times*. "Backs Conviction of Seven Negroes." March 25, 1932.

53. Quoted in *New York Times*. "Backs Conviction of Seven Negroes."

54. Quoted in *New York Times*. "New Trial Ordered by Supreme Court in Scottsboro Case." November 8, 1932, p. 1.

55. *New York Times*. "The Scottsboro Case." November 8, 1932.

56. Quoted in *New York Times*. "New Trial Ordered by Supreme Court in Scottsboro Case."

57. Quoted in Goodman. *Stories of Scottsboro*, p. 87.

58. Quoted in Gilbert Geis and Leigh B. Bienen. *Crimes of the Century*. Boston: Northeastern University Press, 1998, p. 58.

59. Patterson and Conrad. *Scottsboro Boy*, p. 34.

Chapter Four: A Prisoner's World

60. Quoted in Kinshasa. *The Man from Scottsboro*, p. 56.

61. Quoted in Goodman. *Stories of Scottsboro*, p. 91.

62. Quoted in Linder. "The Trials of 'The Scottsboro Boys,'" p. 4.

63. Norris and Washington. *The Last of the Scottsboro Boys*, p. 64.

64. Quoted in Kinshasa. *The Man from Scottsboro*, p. 58.

65. Patterson and Conrad. *Scottsboro Boy*, p. 25.

66. Quoted in Carter. *Scottsboro: A Tragedy of the American South*, p. 166.

67. Quoted in Goodman. *Stories of Scottsboro*, p. 91.

68. Quoted in Goodman. *Stories of Scottsboro*, p. 91.

69. Olen Montgomery. Letter to George Chamlee, May 25, 1931. http://law2.umkc.edu/faculty/projects/FTrials/scottsboro/Montgomery-George.html.

70. Patterson and Conrad. *Scottsboro Boy*, p. 28.

71. Quoted in Quentin Reynolds. *Courtroom: The Story of Samuel S. Leibowitz*. New York: Farrar, Straus, 1950, p. 250.

72. Quoted in Reynolds. *Courtroom*, p. 250.

73. Quoted in Reynolds. *Courtroom*, pp. 251–252.

74. Quoted in Patterson and Conrad. *Scottsboro Boy*, pp. 258–259.

75. *New York Times*. "Scottsboro Trial Moved 50 Miles." March 8, 1933.

76. *New York Times*. "Scottsboro Trial Moved 50 Miles."

Chapter Five: Judge Horton's Courtroom

77. Quoted in F. Raymond Daniell. "Decatur Promises Negroes Fair Play." *New York Times*, March 18, 1933.

78. Quoted in F. Raymond Daniell. "Hunt Girl Witness in Scottsboro Case." *New York Times*, March 26, 1933.

79. Quoted in Acker. *Scottsboro and Its Legacy*, p. 62.

80. Quoted in F. Raymond Daniell. "Girl Repeats Story in Scottsboro Case." *New York Times*, April 4, 1933.

81. Quoted in Carter. *Scottsboro: A Tragedy of the American South*, pp. 210, 223.

82. Quoted in Acker. *Scottsboro and It's Legacy*, p. 74,

83. Quoted in Acker. *Scottsboro and Its Legacy*, p. 74.

84. Quoted in Carter. *Scottsboro: A Tragedy of the American South*, p. 215.

85. Quoted in Carter. *Scottsboro: A Tragedy of the American South*, p. 215.

86. Quoted in Linder. "The Trials of 'The Scottsboro Boys,'" p. 6.

87. Quoted in *Time*. "Races: At Decatur." April 17, 1933, p. 2. www.time.com/time/magazine/article/0,9171,847284,00.html.

88. Quoted in *Time*. "Races: At Decatur," p. 2.

89. Quoted in *Time*. "Races: At Decatur," p. 2.

90. Quoted in F. Raymond Daniell. "New York Attacked in Scottsboro Trial." *New York Times*, April 8, 1933.

91. Quoted in Acker. *Scottsboro and Its Legacy*, p. 90.

92. Quoted in F. Raymond Daniell. "Negro Found Guilty in Scottsboro Case; Jury Out 22 Hours." *New York Times*, April 10, 1933.

93. Quoted in Daniell. "Negro Found Guilty in Scottsboro Case."

94. Quoted in Daniell. "Negro Found Guilty in Scottsboro Case."

95. Quoted in Daniell. "Negro Found Guilty in Scottsboro Case."

96. Quoted in Linder. "The Trials of 'The Scottsboro Boys,'" p. 7.

97. Quoted in Carter. *Scottsboro: A Tragedy of the American South*, pp. 264–265.

98. Quoted in *New York Times*. "Judge Horton Voids Negro's Conviction in Scottsboro Case." June 23, 1933.

99. Norris and Washington. *The Last of the Scottsboro Boys*, pp. 77–78.

100. Patterson and Conrad. *Scottsboro Boy*, p. 48.

101. Quoted in Carter. *Scottsboro: A Tragedy of the American South*, p. 273.

Chapter Six: A New Round of Trials

102. Quoted in Acker. *Scottsboro and Its Legacy*, p. 103.

103. Norris and Washington. *The Last of the Scottsboro Boys*, p. 79.

104. Quoted in Geis and Bienen. *Crimes of the Century*, 1998, p. 67.

105. Patterson and Conrad. *Scottsboro Boy*, p. 49.

106. Norris and Washington. *The Last of the Scottsboro Boys*, p. 143.

107. Quoted in Geis and Bienen. *Crimes of the Century*, 1998, p. 64.

108. Quoted in Acker. *Scottsboro and Its Legacy*, pp. 134–135.

109. Norris and Washington. *The Last of the Scottsboro Boys*, p. 147.

110. Quoted in Acker. *Scottsboro and Its Legacy*, p. 141.

111. Quoted in Acker. *Scottsboro and Its Legacy*, p. 147.

112. Quoted in Acker. *Scottsboro and Its Legacy*, p. 147.
113. Quoted in Acker. *Scottsboro and Its Legacy*, p. 148.
114. Quoted in Crenshaw and Miller. *Scottsboro: The Firebrand of Communism*, p. 258.

Chapter Seven: The Long Ordeal Ends

115. Patterson and Conrad. *Scottsboro Boy*, p. 62.
116. Quoted in F. Raymond Daniell. "Scottsboro Case Goes to the Jury." *New York Times*, January 23, 1936, p. 1.
117. Quoted in Daniell. "Scottsboro Case Goes to the Jury," p. 7.
118. Patterson and Conrad. *Scottsboro Boy*, p. 62.
119. Quoted in Kinshasa. *The Man from Scottsboro*, pp. 121, 124.
120. Quoted in Goodman. *Stories of Scottsboro*, p. 265.
121. Quoted in Goodman. *Stories of Scottsboro*, p. 261.
122. Quoted in Reynolds. *Courtroom: The Story of Samuel S. Leibowitz*, p. 304.
123. Quoted in Carter. *Scottsboro: A Tragedy of the American South*, p. 366.
124. Quoted in F. Raymond Daniell. "Scottsboro Case Ends as 4 Go Free; 2 More Get Prison." *New York Times*, July 25, 1937, p. 4.
125. Quoted in Goodman. *Stories of Scottsboro*, p. 343.
126. Quoted in Carter. *Scottsboro: A Tragedy of the American South*, pp. 382–383.
127. Patterson and Conrad. *Scottsboro Boy*, p. 68.
128. Quoted in Goodman. *Stories of Scottsboro*, p. 350.
129. Quoted in Goodman. *Stories of Scottsboro*, p. 351.
130. Quoted in Goodman. *Stories of Scottsboro*, p. 347.
131. Quoted in Goodman. *Stories of Scottsboro*, p. 368.
132. Quoted in Carter. *Scottsboro: A Tragedy of the American South*, p. 413.
133. Quoted in Carter. *Scottsboro: A Tragedy of the American South*, p. 402.
134. Quoted in Carter. *Scottsboro: A Tragedy of the American South*, p. 402.
135. Quoted in Thomas A. Johnson. "Scottsboro Defendant Applies for a Pardon." *New York Times*, October 9, 1976, p. 1.
136. Norris and Washington. *The Last of the Scottsboro Boys*, p. 147.
137. Quoted in Reynolds. *Courtroom: The Story of Samuel S. Leibowitz*, pp. 313–314.
138. Norris and Washington. frontispiece, *The Last of the Scottsboro Boys*.

For More Information

Books

James R. Acker. *Scottsboro and Its Legacy*. Westport, CT: Praeger, 2008. Acker writes a decent summary of the entire proceedings and includes much material from official court records.

Dan T. Carter. *Scottsboro: A Tragedy of the American South*. Baton Rouge: Louisiana State University Press, 1979. Carter examined all the records and interviewed participants to produce this excellent, readable history.

Files Crenshaw Jr. and Kenneth A. Miller. *Scottsboro: The Firebrand of Communism*. Montgomery, AL: Brown, 1936. Written during the time of the trials, Crenshaw looks at Scottsboro from a southern viewpoint. Although written with a personal and emotional bias, the author nonetheless gives the reader a glimpse into what many Alabama citizens in the 1930s felt.

Gilbert Geis and Leigh B. Bienen. *Crimes of the Century*. Boston: Northeastern University Press, 1998. This book about sensational criminal trials in the country includes a chapter on the Scottsboro trials.

James Goodman. *Stories of Scottsboro.*

New York: Pantheon, 1994. Goodman's book is a well-written companion to Carter's outstanding work. The book is sympathetic to the nine accused.

Arthur Garfield Hays. *Trial by Prejudice*. New York: Civici Friede, 1933. Hays, an attorney who consulted with the defense, explains the early portions of the Scottsboro incident and provides a contrasting view to Crenshaw's book.

Kwando Mbiassi Kinshasa. *The Man from Scottsboro*. Jefferson, NC: McFarland, 1997. Based upon lengthy interviews with Clarence Norris, one of the Scottsboro Nine, this book is a valuable supplement to Norris's autobiography.

League of Struggle for Negro Rights. *They Shall Not Die! The Story of Scottsboro in Pictures*. New York: Workers' Library, 1932. This 1932 pamphlet presents the Communist point of view and is thus heavily laced with propaganda. It is valuable, however, in showing how the Communists utilized the Scottsboro Boys to aid their efforts in attracting new members.

James A. Miller. *Remembering Scottsboro*. Princeton, NJ: Princeton University Press, 2009. Miller examines Scottsboro through the poetry, plays, movies, and books that feature the event as a central theme. He shows how the 1931 incident has remained in the publishing mainstream ever since.

Clarence Norris and Sybil D. Washington. *The Last of the Scottsboro Boys*. New York: G.P. Putnam's Sons, 1979. One of the two autobiographies to emerge from the event, Norris gives the reader a balanced account of what he and the others endured and shows that his decency remained intact despite the horrors thrust upon him.

Haywood Patterson and Earl Conrad. *Scottsboro Boy*. Garden City, NY: Doubleday, 1950. Patterson's autobiography is valuable in conveying his experiences; his personal feelings and anger are evident in the narrative.

Quentin Reynolds. *Courtroom: The Story of Samuel S. Leibowitz*. New York: Farrar, Straus, 1950. This flattering biography of the main defense attorney includes a significant amount of material on Scottsboro as well as Leibowitz's other sensational law cases.

Articles

The following articles were published as the actual events unfolded. Mostly taken from *Time* magazine and the *New York Times*, they give the reader a feel for how people throughout the nation reacted to what occurred in Alabama. They are a superb source for learning about Scottsboro.

From *Time* Magazine

Time. "At Decatur, (Cont'd)." April 17, 1933. www.time.com/time/ magazine/article/0,9171,847284, 00.html.

Time. "Conviction No. 3." December 11, 1933. www.time.com/time/ magazine/article/0,9171,746468,00. html.

Time. "Get It Done Quick." February 3, 1936. www.time.com/time/ magazine/article/0,9171,755726,00. html.

Time. "In Tallapoosa." July 27, 1931. www.time.com/time/magazine/ article/0,9171,752912,00.html.

Time. "Long Journey." July 10, 1950. www.time.com/time/magazine/ article/0,9171,805459,00.html.

Time. "*The Scottsboro Boys*." November 9, 2010. www.time.com/time/specials/ packages/article/0,28804,2023893 _2023892_2028814,00.html.

Time. "Scottsboro Case." June 22, 1931. www.time.com/time/magazine/ article/0,9171,741838,00.html.

Time. "Scottsboro Hero." August 2, 1937. www.time.com/time/magazine/ article/0,9171,770756,00.html.

Time. "Scottsboro Revisited?" October 16, 1978. www.time.com/time/ magazine/article/0,9171,916421, 00.html.

Time. "Seven for Seven." November 14, 1932. www.time.com/time/magazine/ article/0,9171,847039,00.html.

From the *New York Times*

F. Raymond Daniell. "Negro Lad Tells Scottsboro Story." *New York Times*, March 10, 1933.

F. Raymond Daniell. "Scottsboro Case Ends as 4 Go Free; 2 More Get Prison." *New York Times*, July 25, 1937.

F. Raymond Daniell. "Scottsboro Case Goes to the Jury." *New York Times*, January 23, 1936.

F. Raymond Daniell. "Scottsboro Trio Tell of Train Ride." *New York Times*, March 13, 1933.

John Temple Graves II. "Alabama Approves Scottsboro Ruling." *New York Times*, November 8, 1932.

John Temple Graves II. "Alabama Resents Outside Agitation." *New York Times*, June 21, 1931.

Thomas A. Johnson. "Scottsboro Defendant Applies for a Pardon." *New York Times*, October 9, 1976.

New York Times. "Backs Conviction of Seven Negroes." March 25, 1932.

New York Times. "Condemned Negroes Riot in Alabama Jail," April 11, 1931.

New York Times. "Darrow Drops Fight to Save Eight Negroes." December 30, 1931.

New York Times. "Dead Killer Named as Scottsboro Boy," August 18, 1959

New York Times. "Deny Negroes' Trial Is Legal Lynching." April 9, 1931.

New York Times. "8 Negroes Sentenced to Chair in Alabama." April 10, 1931.

New York Times. "Jail Head Asks Troops As Mob Seeks Negroes," March 26, 1931.

New York Times. "New Trial Ordered by Supreme Court in Scottsboro Case." November 8, 1932, pp. 1, 13.

New York Times. "Police Clubs Rout 200 Defiant Reds." April 26, 1931.

New York Times. "The Scottsboro Case." November 8, 1932.

New York Times. "Scottsboro Ruling Evokes Praise Here." November 8, 1932.

New York Times. "Scottsboro Trial Begins Tomorrow." March 5, 1933

New York Times. "Scottsboro Trial Moved 50 Miles." March 8, 1933.

New York Times. "Supreme Justices Get Scottsboro Appeals." May 28, 1932.

Other Articles

Hollace Ransdell. "Report on the Scottsboro, Ala. Case." American Civil Liberties Union, May 27, 1931. www.law.umkc.edu/faculty/projects/FTrials/scottsboro/Scottsororeport.pdf.

Mary Heaton Vorse. "How Scottsboro Happened." *New Republic*, May 10, 1933, pp. 1–5. www.marxists.org/subject/women/authors/vorse/scotts.html.

Websites

Famous American Trials (http://law2.umkc.edu/faculty/projects/FTrials/scottsboro/scottsb.htm). This website contains a wide variety of information about the trials. It includes brief biographies of the main participants, excerpts from court transcripts, photographs, a map, a chronology, and other fascinating material.

Scottsboro: An American Tragedy (www.pbs.org/wgbh/amex/scottsboro/ filmmore/ps_wright.html). From PBS, which produced the documentary, this excellent website includes a transcript of the program, a timeline, a teacher's guide to additional activities, and more.

Scottsboro Stories (http://scottsboro stories.blogspot.com/). This revealing website is devoted not only to the story of the Scottsboro Boys but also to developing an understanding of different cultures and creating cultural diversity.

Index

Picture Credits

Cover: © Bettmann/Corbis
AFP/Getty Images, 11
Andrew H. Walker/Getty Images, 112
Bettmann/Corbis, 10, 14, 18, 24, 33, 43, 57, 60, 71, 75, 77, 79, 82, 88, 98
Charles Hoff/NY Daily News Archive via Getty images, 44
John Tresilian/NY Daily News Archive via Getty Images, 50
Keystone-France/Gamma-Keystone via Getty Images, 31, 54
Marion Post Wolcott/Library of Congress/Getty Images, 7
MPI/Getty Images, 36, 94
Nate Parsons/The Washington Post/Getty Images, 111
NY Daily News Archive via Getty Images, 29, 53, 63, 66, 68, 85, 92, 95, 103, 106
© Underwood & Underwood/Corbis, 40-41

About the Author

John F. Wukovits is a retired junior high school teacher and writer from Trenton, Michigan, who specializes in history and biography. Besides biographies of Anne Frank, Jim Carrey, Michael J. Fox, Stephen King, and Martin Luther King Jr. for Lucent, he has written biographies of the World War II commander Admiral Clifton Sprague, Barry Sanders, Tim Allen, Jack Nicklaus, Vince Lombardi, and Wyatt Earp. He is also the author of many books about World War II, including the July 2003 book *Pacific Alamo: The Battle for Wake Island*, the August 2006 *One Square Mile of Hell: The Battle for Tarawa*, the November 2006 *Eisenhower: A Biography*, and the June 2009 volume *American Commando*, about Marine Colonel Evans Carlson and his Marine Raiders. A graduate of the University of Notre Dame, Wukovits is the father of three daughters—Amy, Julie, and Karen—and the grandfather of Matthew, Megan, Emma, and Kaitlyn.